# WALT CRAWFORD

# FIRST HAVE SOMETHING TO SAY

*Writing for the Library Profession*

**AMERICAN LIBRARY ASSOCIATION**
Chicago    2003

Portions of chapter 9 originally appeared in different form as parts of "The E-Files: 'You *Must* Read This': Library Weblogs," *American Libraries* 32 (October 2001). 74–76, and "The E-Files: Library Lists: Building on E-Mail," *American Libraries* 32 (November 2001): 56–58.

Portions of chapter 10 originally appeared in different form as parts of "The E-Files: E-Newsletters and E-Zines: From Current Cites to NewBreed Librarian," *American Libraries* 32 (December 2001): 51–53.

The first part of chapter 15 originally appeared in slightly different form as "disContent: Give Me a Break!," *EContent* 25 (April 2002): 42–43.

Design and composition by ALA Editions in Berkeley Book and Benguiat using Quark-XPress 5 on a PC platform

Printed on 50-pound white offset, a pH-neutral stock, and bound in 10-point cover stock by Victor Graphics

The paper used in this publication meets the minimum requirements of American National Standard for Information Sciences—Permanence of Paper for Printed Library Materials, ANSI Z39.48-1992. ∞

**Library of Congress Cataloging-in-Publication Data**

Crawford, Walt.
First have something to say : writing for the library profession / Walt Crawford.
p. cm.
Includes bibliographical references and index.
ISBN 0-8389-0851-9
1. Library science—Authorship. 2. Library science literature—Publishing.
3. Communication in library science. 4. Authorship—Marketing. I. Title.
Z665.C776 2003
808'.006602—dc21                                          2003004113

Printed in the United States of America

07  06  05  04  03        5  4  3  2  1

# CONTENTS

*Contents*

# PREFACE

**N**othing I say here should be taken as revealed truth or the only way to proceed. I hope to convince you that there is no single way to proceed—that your path should be individual, and that you shouldn't focus too much on maintaining a path.

Some elements of this guide run counter to conventional wisdom. Others conflict with received library wisdom, as I understand it. When I'm aware of that, I'll provide a suitable flag: "Heresy alert."

## Acknowledgments

I can't begin to name everyone who encouraged me to write and speak or who helped improve the results. A few names and sources come to mind, but memory lapses ensure that many others—some of them possibly more important—don't appear here. My apologies to those not named.

Susan K. Martin encouraged me to write my first published article, "Building a Serials Key Word Index," when she directed the Library Systems Office at the University of California–Berkeley's Doe Library. That was my only publication while working in that office, but that's not Sue's fault. I've treasured her friendship ever since, as she moved from Berkeley to continue an illustrious career. She was also editor of the *Journal of Library Automation* (*JOLA*) at the time—but since I was a member of the Library and Information Technology Association (LITA, or, at the time, ISAD) first and foremost, *JOLA* was my natural outlet in any case.

Brian Aveny, editor of *JOLA* and its successor, *Information Technology and Libraries* (*ITAL*), during the transitional period of the early 1980s, nagged me into preparing the article "Long Searches, Slow Response: Recent Experience on RLIN" in 1983. In his comments in *ITAL*'s silver anniversary issue (12:1, March 1993—the silver anniversary included the thirteen years of *JOLA*), he notes his pride in that nagging "less because of its content than because it was the first publication by one of today's most prolific library automation writers." That *JOLA* article was actually my eighth publication and third real article—but it was my first article based on work at RLG, and may have marked the point at which I began to take writing seriously.

On the book side, I owe an unpayable debt to two groups who are necessarily nameless: (1) people who needed to understand MARC better in the early 1980s, and who wound up talking to me as one of RLG's experienced MARC people, convincing me that the field needed a publication to improve understanding of the formats; and (2) the real experts in MARC, none of whom had the time or the interest to write such a book, finally leading me to a "What the heck" decision to do it myself.

Knowledge Industry Publications, Inc., took a chance on this book by an unknown writer on a topic they didn't understand after ALA Editions had dithered over a decision for many months. Looking back at that first book, which was published in 1984, I am reminded of early personal computing: it was prepared on a Morrow MD2, running CP/M with 128K of memory and a grand total of 720K storage in the form of two diskette drives. (Operating system and applications on one diskette, data on the other.) Hard disk? Not in those days, not with my budget. I used WordStar, which worked surprisingly well on that puny little machine.

Ed Wall of the Pierian Press played a long, encouraging role in my move from occasional article writer to steady contributor. I'm not sure who first suggested submitting "Commonsense System Pricing; or, How Much Will That $1,200 Computer Really Cost?" (*Library Hi Tech* 2:2, 1984), but I knew that it was not suitable for *ITAL*—and somehow that single article turned into a series of fifty articles between 1984 and 1998 and a related series of fifty-nine "newsletters within a newsletter" in *Library Hi Tech News* between 1995 and 2000—the first time I met a monthly schedule.

Kathleen (Kathy) Bales, a dear friend and colleague for more than two decades, conspired with my wife to convince me to apply to edit the *LITA Newsletter*, which was a remarkable learning experience between 1985 and 1994. Charles W. Bailey Jr. invited me to join the *Public-Access Computer Systems Review* editorial board in 1989, my first experience with an electronic journal.

Finally, my special thanks to the Arizona State Library Association's Library Automation Round Table. Their invitation to speak at the association's annual conference was neither my first speech nor my first invited speech—but it was the first time an invitation came without a specific topic, resulting in my first speech on the death of print and other nonsense. Bewildered attendees at some of my disorganized keynote addresses may be less grateful to this group.

Thanks to the editors who have cleaned up my prose during the decades. Readers of *Cites & Insights: Crawford at Large* should appreciate the difference good editing makes, since they see my handiwork without editorial oversight.

I don't think I could do any of this without the support and inspiration of my wife, the real librarian in our household, Linda A. Driver. I had precisely one publication and no speeches before marrying Linda. Who knows? If I hadn't met her, by now I might have three articles and two speeches to my credit.

# 1

## Why Write?

The best reason to write or speak is right there in the title of this book: because you have something to say. More to the point, you have something to share—something to say that other people will want to read or hear. That's at the heart of almost all good writing and speaking.

One common motive for writing and speaking is to gain tenure or promotion. There's nothing wrong with this as one of the reasons you write. As the only reason, it's unfortunate and tends to be obvious. When you write or speak because it's required, and only for that reason, your articles and speeches are likely to reflect that mandate. I've read too many journal articles that fairly shout "I wrote this for tenure": loaded with literature surveys and footnotes, good enough to pass peer review, and either empty or much less interesting than a good article should be.

I'm aware that many academic librarians and most library school faculty need publications for tenure or promotion. Can you set that need aside for a while, to discover your other reasons for writing? If so, you'll probably write more interesting articles and enjoy the process more. When you enjoy the process and produce interesting articles, it's likely that you'll keep writing. That's good for your career and even better for your mental health and the health of the profession.

What holds for writing also holds for speaking—but many people find public speaking far more difficult than writing, and you're likely to see fewer indirect benefits from speaking, since it's tough to cite a speech or "republish" someone else's speech ten years later. To be a good speaker, you must not only have something to say, you must care about it enough to overcome the psychological barriers.

## The Wrong Reasons

If you're planning to make big bucks in the library writing and speaking game, think again. Maybe you've heard about six-figure advances for books and five-figure fees for speeches. I can't swear that no librarian receives five-figure honoraria, but most often that's only true if you ignore the decimal point. And six-figure advances for books don't happen in a field where 5,000 copies over two years constitute a best-seller.

Profit may be the dumbest motive for becoming a library writer or speaker. If you're a superbly talented writer who is only in it for the money, turn your hand to biography, motivational works, high-profile children's literature—not library writing.

Chances are, much of your early writing won't earn you a dime. Journals almost never pay authors. Smaller magazines rarely pay authors. If you contribute a chapter to a book, a copy of the book may be the closest you get to a fee. Most library books begin with a modest advance (or no advance at all) and pay modest royalties—not because the publishers are crooks, but because the market is small. For the same reasons, even publications that do pay for articles probably won't pay much. A good target for freelance writers is a dollar a word minimum. With the exception of one unusual speech, I've *never* received that much for writing or speaking, and rarely half that.

As an experienced and fairly prolific library writer, you may earn a nice bit of extra income. If you're a superb trainer with a distinctive message, you might even earn a living this way—but most of that living will come from workshops and the like, not from writing.

If profit is the silliest motive for library writing, fame and glory may not be far behind. Not that you can't achieve some fame through writing—you can, as I can attest. But if you set out to do so, you're likely to fail. Readers can spot the writer who's trying too hard. So can the best editors.

## That Driving Urge

You feel the need to express yourself, and you have something to say that people need to read or hear. Much of this book will deal with some of those "somethings" and their natural venues. Consider some of the things you may have to say:

> You've done research that yielded worthwhile results for use by other libraries and librarians. This is the classic basis for a journal article and the start of many library writing careers.

Reviewing the existing literature on a topic, you've seen correlations and consequences that nobody's mentioned up to now. Putting the pieces together, you can create new knowledge out of existing information.

As you read current articles on a topic outside the library field, you see that librarians need to know about this topic—and you can tell them about it in ways that make sense to them and speak to their needs.

You're creating something new that librarians need to know about—or you're working with others to make a new service work better.

You attended a conference and were inspired by some of the sessions. You'd like to spread the word to those who weren't at the conference.

Your own work leads you to doubt something you see as common knowledge in the literature. You feel the need to argue with that common knowledge, maybe even show it up as based on bad information or clumsy thinking.

You haven't read an article on an important topic that explains the topic sensibly or thoroughly—and you believe you can do better.

These are a few good reasons to start writing or speaking. In every case, the first motive is that you have something to say—something that you haven't seen said as well or to the same audience.

## Becoming a Writer

This is the point at which I should start pronouncing the rules of good writing, giving you the lessons you need to make your articles sing and make editors jump with joy when they see your submissions.

Fortunately for the reader, there is no single best approach to writing. If every library writer wrote in the same way, the results would be even drearier than today's third-tier journals. If you intend to write more than journal articles, or if you want your journal articles to be read and appreciated, you need to develop your own style. That doesn't mean you can't seek out and use advice. It does mean you should retain personality in your writing.

### Mechanics and Mathematics

I can offer a few words about mechanics and mathematics. The mechanics should be obvious these days, but I know they're not. You need access to a computer with good word-processing software (either Microsoft Word or software that produces Word-compatible files) and a letter-quality printer. You need good-quality white paper, which means anything from standard copier paper on up.

Plan to submit most items double spaced, without hyphenation, with at least one-inch margins on all sides, with page numbers—unless the publication you're writing for explicitly asks for electronic submission, which typically means sending Word files as e-mail attachments.

Early on, plan to include a self-addressed stamped envelope with every paper submission. Things get more casual when you're more established, particularly if you say "Just send me e-mail and recycle the paper if you can't use this." Don't get too fancy with your typography, your style, or (particularly) your paper. A clean 12-point serif typeface such as Times New Roman always works well and plain white paper is really the only way to go.

If you have headings, include them. Many writers don't, leaving that step to editors—but headings help organize an article, and most editors would rather work with your headings than start from scratch.

Learn to spell. Don't rely on spell-checkers. They can't handle cases where the wrong word is spelled correctly.

Learn the basics of grammar. Word's grammar checker does surprisingly well, but it's no substitute for understanding grammar.

Read enough to understand some of the most common mistakes—its and it's, there and their, discreet and discrete, and a few dozen others.

Far be it from me to tell you to understand punctuation thoroughly, since I never have—but do pay attention to the way quotations are handled in the country where you publish. In America, commas and periods always come before the closing quote marks (largely for typographic reasons), while colons and semicolons always follow the closing quotes. Exclamation points and question marks are, uniquely and necessarily, used logically: before the closing quote if they're part of the quotation itself, after if they relate to the sentence that includes the quotation. In Britain, the rules are different—as, incidentally, are the hyphenation rules.

You may find yourself breaking some traditional rules for grammar and for writing, such as sentences ending with prepositions or beginning with conjunctions, sentence fragments, and inappropriate contractions. I'm a great believer in breaking the rules when that improves communication or flow, but you need to know the rules before you start breaking them.

If you're writing about statistics and numbers, learn enough to get your facts right. Nothing can be "200 percent cheaper" or "take 150 percent less time." There's so much to say about numeracy and the proper use of statistics—most of it inappropriate for this book—that I'll stop here, with one exception: "An order of magnitude" does not mean "lots"—it means either ten times larger or more numerous or one-tenth as large or numerous.

## The Usual Suspects

You've probably read at least one serious guide to style already. If you haven't, there's no shortage of standard guides—and no shortage of reasons to question their advice.

Take the classic, *The Elements of Style* by William Strunk Jr. and E. B. White. It's short, clear, and unambiguous. It can also cripple your writing if you take it too seriously.

Consider *The Elements of Expression* by Arthur Plotnik, former editor of *American Libraries*. I own a signed first edition (Holt, 1996), which I read in its entirety. Enjoyed it, too, for the most part. Do I agree with everything Plotnik says? Not a chance. Will it help you move from the basics of clear writing to a better understanding of expression? Probably.

If you're nervous about your writing ability, you'll benefit from reading either of these books or any of a dozen others. Go to a good independent bookstore, and look at handbooks on good writing. See which ones strike you as clearly written and interesting. Buy one and read it as a starting point.

Borrow a couple more from your library. Keep writing while you're reading about writing, just as any good writer keeps reading to write. At some point, probably within two or three books, you'll start to disagree with some of the advice and know why you're disagreeing—or you'll point to a paragraph, say "I can write better than that," and proceed to do so.

Read some articles and essays by Michael Gorman. Read one or two of my columns and articles. We may both be established writers, but we have wildly different styles. Now try to figure out the merged style in *Future Libraries: Dreams, Madness, and Reality,* a book we coauthored.

After you have a modest track record as a writer, pick up another guide to good writing or try rereading your old standbys. See whether the advice still makes sense. Test the new guides against your own knowledge. Unless you're unhappy with your progress, don't do that too often. Reading to write is vital, but reading too much about writing can stifle your own style.

Art Plotnik includes a lengthy annotated set of resources at the back of *The Elements of Expression*. I particularly like his suggestion that you read one or more of the *It Was a Dark and Stormy Night* series—winning entries from the Bulwer-Lytton bad writing contest. Reading paragraphs judged to be the worst possible writing can be entertaining and useful—even though there's reason to prefer over-the-top awfulness to the blandness that characterizes so much library writing.

## My Writing Heroes

I miss Isaac Asimov. I don't claim him as a role model, but I do admire the clarity of his prose and use it as a goal for my own nonfiction. I'll never have his explanatory abilities, his range (he wrote about almost everything, although he had a short list of topics he did not write on), his output, or (for that matter) his reputation as a mild-mannered dirty old man. If I can achieve a fraction of Asimov's clarity, I'll be satisfied. But I do not aim to duplicate Asimov's style.

I aim for plain English but usually find myself avoiding the choppiness of short, simple sentences. I don't use a thesaurus (and I'm sure it shows) but also don't aim for eighth-grade readability. Somehow, I've managed to create a number of pithy sayings over the years—but never intentionally.

That's me. You're you. You don't want my style. You want to build your own.

## Journals and Magazines

I've already drawn a distinction between journals and magazines, and that distinction will be made throughout this book. Here's the difference between the two, at least as I use the terms.

A *journal* consists primarily of scholarly papers concerning aspects of the journal's topic area, typically without payment to the authors and most commonly with peer review of the manuscripts. Ideally, peer review is double-blind (the authors don't know who's reviewing their papers and the reviewers don't know who wrote a paper).

A *magazine* consists of articles rather than scholarly papers and is more likely to include a mix of solicited or commissioned articles, contributed articles, and staff-written articles. Many magazines pay writers for their articles.

When every article ends with footnotes, there's a good chance you're dealing with a journal. The differences can be fuzzy, as both periodical forms can include columns, topical clusters, reviews, and other elements.

## Why Not Write?

If every library professional wrote and published one article a year, we'd have our own internal serials crisis. Most people in the field never publish—and most published writers stop at one or two articles. If you plan to write one article and stop, you're reading this book for amusement.

There are other hobbies, most of them more fun and more social. You don't need to write to make a name for yourself in the library field. You don't need to publish to be a well-rounded professional.

But you have something to say and an urge to be heard.

Why not write?

# 2

## Getting Started
### *Room for One More*

**B**reaking into library writing isn't like breaking into major league baseball or getting your library admitted to the Association of Research Libraries. There's always room for one more writer who has something to say and cares about what they're saying. Many publications welcome new writers, with editors always looking for people who can communicate effectively. You're likely to find that even big-name library publications are approachable—a lesson I learned twenty years late.

If you've been reading mainstream writing advice such as *Writer's Monthly*, be aware that things work a little differently with most library publishers.

For example, don't even think about finding an agent. You can't afford one on your receipts from library writing. You don't need one for your submissions to be read. Many library publishers, including book publishers, don't work with agents.

You don't need to work your way up step by step. My first book appeared after a mere six publications (only three of them articles) and was related to only one of those six. I've known others who published a book with even fewer publications. I'm almost certain that people have appeared in *American Libraries* and *Library Journal* with no prior formal publications.

There may be publications that will offer you assignments with near-guaranteed publication, but that hasn't been my experience. While many articles are solicited, many others come "over the transom," i.e., they are submitted without prior contact. Through 2001, only one of my *American Libraries* articles was arranged in advance—and in 2000, more than half the articles I submitted to *American Libraries* were rejected.

# Starting Out Slowly

If you already have something to say that's important enough for a first-tier journal or one of the major library magazines, *go for it.* If you're planning on writing for the long term and aren't ready to start at the top, you can try several approaches to build your confidence and establish a reputation before aiming for the big leagues. Just don't be surprised when the big leagues turn out to be the same as the smaller outfits.

## Writing at Work: Honing Your Skills

Who doesn't need to write at work? If you think of committee reports, proposals, drafts, and other work requirements as writing opportunities, and not just as bureaucratic overhead, they provide valuable practice for your writing skills. There's a danger, of course: if you do a spectacular job on your work documents, they may unnerve readers who expect the usual soothing drone.

## In-House Writing beyond Assignments

Does your library or organization have a staff newsletter? Write for it. The expectations here usually don't equal those for a national publication and you can work on your writing with a smaller audience.

Don't let expectations govern performance. I can think of at least two good reasons to aim for the same quality in a house newsletter article that you'd strive for in a book chapter or major article:

1. *Pride and professionalism.* No good reference librarian settles for a half-right answer because the person asking the question isn't a likely major donor. No good cataloger settles for mediocre work because the book in question will never be read. Why would your writing differ in this regard? Why would you settle for mediocrity simply because the readership is limited?

2. *Unexpected opportunities.* Is anyone on your staff prominent in the field, on an editorial board or two, or otherwise in a position to point you out to others? Are you sure? Even if everyone on your staff is obscure and intends to remain that way, you can never tell where copies of your in-house publication might wind up. When you have a bylined article that sparkles with thought and creativity, there's always a chance that someone will see it who can and will help you move forward.

That's idealistic, of course. In-house publications usually involve odd deadlines and tough length limits, not uncommonly have multiple review rounds, and impose house styles that prevent you from doing your best. Still, I've seen some superb pieces appearing in library newsletters from people I'd never known as writers. They didn't settle for in-house mediocrity; neither should you.

How about in-house writing that goes outside? That's your first step toward writing for a broader audience. Whether it's the best way to move outside your institution is another question, one that depends on local politics and habits. Most staff publications also go outside the library, but that's incidental. Publications planned for broader distribution take on a different character, and that character may require a rigid style and approach. If you have the opportunity to write about work-related issues for that broader audience, that's all to the good. But there are times when in-house publications can be the toughest publications to write for.

I've written for RLG's widely distributed newsletter off and on over the years, as work projects have made it desirable or editors have requested articles. It's been enlightening and frustrating (at times) to deal with the editorial issues in this sort of publication.

As I wrote the first draft of this book, one of my articles ("Connecting Citations and Full Text: Eureka® and OpenURL") was the lead piece in the current issue of *RLG Focus,* followed by three related articles from RLG members using OpenURL. I worked as hard on that article as I would on an *American Libraries* column and I'm proud of the results—but I'm more delighted by the trio of first-rate member contributions. Links to those articles are already appearing elsewhere, suggesting that they'll have significant impact. That's a bonus for in-house writing, and it's one I've seen at many institutions, as their publications (particularly those available in electronic form) reach far beyond the walls.

"Sure, I recognize your name. You wrote a great piece in Wossamatta University Library's quarterly last year." Don't expect it—but don't be surprised when it happens.

## Local Outlets

Beyond your own library, consider local, state, and regional possibilities. Does your state library association have a newsletter? The editor's probably hungry for submissions. The association may be hungry for an editor, for that matter—a topic I take up later, but one good way to gain confidence as a library writer.

## Conference Reporting

Is it possible to have too many good conference reports? There can surely be too many boring reports that tell you who spoke and the institutions they represented, summarize the bullet points from the inevitable PowerPoint presentation, and offer no insight into the meaning of what was said. If you can rise above such hackwork, you can go far with conference reports even as a beginning writer—for your staff newsletter, for local library publications, and for national and international publications.

When I edited the *LITA Newsletter*, I encouraged newcomers to sign up for conference program reporting and accommodated those newcomers by expanding the publication and adopting an editorial style that kept the writer's voice intact. I believe I brought at least a dozen new people into the library writing game.

The *LITA Newsletter* is gone, but there are many other venues for conference reports. *Library Hi Tech News* explicitly opens its pages for conference-report submissions from newcomers and experienced writers alike. So do many other print and electronic publications.

The most common form of conference report may be the dry-as-dust "he said, she said, they said" program account. These can be valuable—but less so today, when conference planners can mount PowerPoint slide shows directly on the Web. You can do better. To my mind, the best conference reports come in two flavors, both of which honor the conference by adding insight to pure reporting:

1. *Interpretive program reports* work from the presentations in one or more programs and build context around those presentations. These reports craft new stories from the raw material of the programs, synthesizing new meaning and adding the writer's voice.

2. *Conference-wide reports* start from the reporter's overall experience, mixing receptions, exhibits, friends, and program themes into a whole with meaning of its own. Even badly done all-conference reports can be fascinating. The best ones are works of art and leave readers regretting that they missed the conference, but happy that they gained so much meaning from something they didn't see.

My sense is that most established writers don't go back to conference reporting. That's a shame, although I can understand why. Good conference reporting falls somewhere between journalism and essay or traditional article writing. It can build your skills while providing a service to your readers. Remember that even with the American Library Association's Annual

Conference, nine out of ten librarians didn't attend the conference. No matter what the conference, chances are that most of your readers didn't attend the programs you enjoyed or hated.

## Moving On

Work reports, staff newsletters, articles in library publications, pieces in the newsletters of local library associations, conference reports. These are all great ways to get started. You can establish a fair reputation if you do a superior job here. You can also get started by reviewing books, which is discussed at length in chapter 7.

At some point, you'll probably feel the need to move on: to tell your own stories at greater length to a broader audience, in a journal, some other publication, a book, or through some other means.

If you start out with these earlier steps, you may already have established a style and an approach. That style and approach will probably change as you move on.

# 3

## Journals
### *Tell Me Something New*

**R**efereed scholarly journals: *Information Technology and Libraries, College & Research Libraries, RQ, Journal of the American Society for Information Science,* and dozens (or hundreds?) of others in librarianship and information science, at least fifteen or twenty thousand in science, technology, and medicine.

Those three words—"refereed scholarly journal"—give fledgling and established authors nightmares while also representing the presumed peak of professional writing. You've been published in a major journal: what could be better or more terrifying?

## Demystifying the Journals

Neither the mystique nor the terror of refereed journals makes much sense in librarianship unless your primary goal is to be part of the scholarly apparatus. If you plan a varied writing career and hope to have a good reputation, and particularly if you're in an academic library, you will probably publish more than one refereed paper in a scholarly journal. If you're successful, those papers probably won't be your most important publications as measured by their impact on the field, although they may have the most citations in scholarly papers.

*Heresy alert:* What I've just said deviates from the whole scholarly culture. As with most cultures, formal scholarship tends to be inbred. We're taught that the measure of a journal's importance is its citation density—the rate at which its articles are cited in other scholarly journals. More than that, the measure of a scholar is both the number of refereed articles and the number of citations to those articles (presumably excluding self-citations).

If you're a library school professor or plan to be one, the inbred scholarly attitude may serve you well. It's certainly true that some journals in the library field seem dominated by library school faculty and graduate students, possibly for reasons that may become evident later in this discussion. But librarianship is more than an academic field, and the library field includes more than professional librarians (or I couldn't be writing this book!). Librarians and library staff need more than journal articles and read more than refereed scholarly journals; most library people probably spend more time reading (and learn more from) library magazines, newsletters, and electronic services than they do reading the formal journals in the field.

The nightmares are also overblown. Referees are other library people with some background in the journal's topical area. They—we—are neither gods nor infallible. In my experience on both sides of the process, most referees want to see writers succeed. They're looking for articles that inform and improve the field and for ways to improve articles that aren't quite ready, not for excuses to reject submissions.

Although submission and rejection rates vary, most library-related journals these days don't have dozens of submissions for each available article slot. Many editors are always looking for good new articles. In practice, many journals publish manuscripts that don't qualify as scholarly refereed articles—although the best ones always clearly distinguish between refereed articles and other material.

## Good Places to Start

Am I saying you should skip refereed scholarly journals and look elsewhere for your first big publication? Not really—or at least not always. If you're an academic librarian, and in some other cases, there may be good reasons to make your first formal publication an article in a refereed scholarly journal. For example:

1. Proper blind reviewing means that established names don't have an advantage over newcomers. Your name isn't attached to your manuscript. If you can write, have something new to offer, and meet the other requirements of scholarly writing, your chances are theoretically equal to those of the most widely published authors.

2. If you can meet the requirements and follow the forms of a scholarly journal, you demonstrate significant organizational and research ability, as

well as writing ability. These are traits that will serve you well in other writing venues.

3. Premier and second-tier journals do help to establish your reputation. That will help you gain acceptance for other forms of writing and may lead to invitations from editors of journals that don't rely on submissions.

My first nonlocal publication in the library field was a refereed article, "Building a Serials Key Word Index," which appeared in the *Journal of Library Automation* in March 1976, just a year after I joined the American Library Association (ALA). My next refereed article came eight years later, and there have been perhaps half a dozen others since then. I didn't begin to think of library writing as a serious ongoing interest until 1984, when my second refereed article, first book, and first three articles in an ongoing series appeared.

Two articles in eight years? That's pathetic for a scholar—but it's better than average for a practitioner, and it obviously didn't set the pace for my future writing.

I believe the formal article was a good starting point, and at the time I was working in an academic library, though not in a tenure-track position. I know that first submission was unnerving and may have been partly responsible for my slowness in beginning regular writing. I also know that many good writers begin with a refereed scholarly article or two.

The rest of this chapter quotes segments of the "*ITAL* Instructions to Authors" as of June 19, 2002 (available at www.lita.org/ital/infoauth.htm). Every professionally run refereed scholarly journal has a set of instructions for authors. You should always read or download those instructions before submitting an article to a journal. The instructions for *Information Technology and Libraries* (*ITAL*) are fairly typical—and, of course, if you're writing in areas that *ITAL* covers, I urge you to consider submitting articles to my "home journal."

## The Review Process: Learning from Feedback

Here's what the *ITAL* instructions say about the review process:

> *ITAL* is a refereed journal using double-blind reviewing. The editor assigns manuscripts to reviewers who receive the manuscript with no direct information on the author or the author's affiliation. Reviewers examine the manuscript considering the following:
>
> • Is the topic within the scope of *ITAL?*

- Is it meaningful and relevant to *ITAL* readers?
- Does it offer something to the literature?
- Is it timely?
- Is the presentation that of an article or merely the text of an oral presentation?
- Is it organized well? Does it have a point?
- Are the citations complete and accurate?

Upon completing the review, a recommendation is presented to the editor as to the suitability of the manuscript for publication in *ITAL*. Recommendations fall into one of the following categories:

- Publishable in its current condition
- Significant and sound and should be published with only minor editorial revisions
- Basically significant and sound but requires some rewriting to make it a solid publishable contribution
- Requires major rewriting, and it should be reviewed again after a revised draft has been received
- Does not warrant publication as a full article but might be published as a "Communication"
- Does not warrant further consideration by *ITAL*

The author is informed of the recommendation and any comments made by the reviewers. The review process takes six to eight weeks.

Consider the first two sentences. "Double-blind reviewing" means that the reviewers or referees don't know who wrote the article or, directly, what their affiliation is—and the author won't know who reviewed the article. Double-blind reviewing offers the only transparent method for evaluating manuscripts. "Peer review" doesn't always mean double-blind review—but I'll get to that later.

*Heresy alert:* Double blindness only goes so far. Many articles leave no doubt as to the institutional affiliation of the author(s), and there's no way to avoid that short of a rewriting process that no library-related journal could possibly afford. Some authors have styles so distinctive (or such egregious amounts of self-citation) that there's little doubt in any experienced reviewer's mind as to who wrote the article at hand.

Nonetheless, when I've reviewed submissions to *ITAL*, I have *never* correctly guessed the author. On those occasions where I (mistakenly) thought

I recognized the author, I don't believe it influenced my judgment. In fact, it was more likely to be a case of "I wish my old friend Jill Schmo hadn't written such an awful article," or "Who knew that idiot Jack Schmoo could do such good work?"

Now consider the rest of the quoted section of the *ITAL* instructions. Every journal has a scope and a primary readership. If you're out of scope or your article doesn't speak to the readership, you won't get published.

"Does it offer something to the literature?" and "Is it timely?" are other ways of saying, "Tell me something new." If you don't have something new to add to the literature, you don't belong in scholarly journals—and reviewers may look for a demonstration that you know you have something new, e.g., a literature review.

A note here about "deli publication"—slicing a research project's results into thin little articles so that the project yields four, six, a dozen articles. If you read many scholarly journals in almost any field, you've seen deli publications, typically with thinly sliced results spread across a variety of journals. (The resulting articles are sometimes called "least publishable units.") It's an effective way to pad a publication record. It's also unfortunate for writer and reader alike—the writer because it vitiates the impact of the research (and will eventually breed cynicism about the writer's articles), the reader because it's harder to understand and appreciate the full scope of the research. This is not to say that a single project should always yield only a single article, but that articles should not proliferate simply because it's feasible. "Tell me something new" should mean just that—not "tell me something that's a tiny bit different than what I already know."

The next bullet makes an important point: a written speech is not a formal article, although it can be turned into one.

The final bullet notes one key aspect of scholarly articles. Most have citations, many have literature reviews, and completeness and accuracy in both areas count.

The remainder of the instructions deserves attention as well, since good reviewers can help you improve your writing and research. When reviewers offer a recommendation other than the first or last, comments usually accompany the recommendation. Good reviewers don't offer comments lightly, and double-blind reviewing means reviewers have no reason to crush your spirit or puff up your ego.

*ITAL* typically uses two reviewers for an article. Think of those reviewers as unpaid editors. If you're serious about writing, you should welcome advice from editors—and you should welcome advice from reviewers. If you're lucky, you may find that editors and reviewers help you recognize and eliminate the most common flaws in your writing while emphasizing your strengths.

# Form and Formalism

The submission instructions for *Information Technology and Libraries* are also fairly typical for journals using mailed review processes:

1. Submit original, unpublished manuscripts only. Do not submit a manuscript being considered for publication elsewhere. Authors are responsible for the accuracy of the information in the manuscript, including references, statistics, and URLs.

2. Manuscripts should be machine-printed and double-spaced. Two copies should be provided. It is not necessary to provide the manuscript in electronic format until it has been accepted for publication. Author name, title, and affiliation should appear on a separate cover page only. This information should not be repeated in the text of manuscript, or in the abstract. Pages should be numbered. An abstract of 100 words or less should be provided on a separate sheet.

3. *ITAL* follows the *Chicago Manual of Style,* 14th edition, for capitalization, punctuation, quotations, tables, captions, and elements of bibliographic style, including references. Spelling will follow *Webster's Collegiate Dictionary,* 10th edition.

4. Information on submission of electronic copy, tables and illustrations, copyright forms, and other aspects of a final copy will be provided when a manuscript has been accepted for publication.

While details will differ for other journals and the instructions will be significantly different for journals with electronic review processes, key elements apply to most journals. These include the following:

Most journals do not accept previously published material and don't accept multiple submissions. The definition of "published" varies considerably, and there are exceptions, but this is the norm.

The journal is not in a position to correct your references, statistics, or other facts.

You already know that you should have a double-spaced style as one option for submission, whether printed or as an electronic document. For reviewing and copyediting purposes, double-spaced text is simply easier to work with, particularly for editorial annotation.

Other provisions of the second paragraph make blind reviewing possible: your manuscript *must not* include your name and affiliation in the body of the text.

Always follow the style required by the journal. *Chicago* is the most common (and probably most straightforward) style, but there are hundreds of other styles. If you don't want to buy a copy of the *Chicago Manual of Style,* every good library has it. Spelling should be consistent in most American dictionaries—and there are many cases where your Word or other spell-checker won't catch errors.

Some journals provide full details for final submission up front. Some don't. You'll probably be asked to submit final copy in machine-readable form, most commonly as a Word attachment in e-mail.

Scholarly journal articles are more formal than most other forms of publication. You'll probably include a literature review, as well as footnotes or endnotes, and possibly both. You should plan to use fewer abbreviations and a more formal style than I use here.

Formality does not mean abandoning your voice. It does mean finding a happy medium between your voice and the requirements of a formal article. Formality does not always mean spending half your space on an exhaustive (exhausting?) literature review; it does mean providing such a review when it's necessary to provide background for your message or to prove its relevance and newness.

Many journal editors—in my opinion, all *good* journal editors—will compromise on formality when it doesn't damage the integrity, organization, or message of your article. Most editors will not and should not compromise on the form in which an article is submitted. They've stated the rules; you should follow them.

## Understanding the Journal

*Information Technology and Libraries* publishes material related to all aspects of libraries and information technology, including digital libraries, metadata, authorization and authentication, electronic journals and electronic publishing, telecommunications, distributed systems and networks, computer security and intellectual property rights, technical standards, geographic information systems, desktop applications, online catalogs and bibliographic systems, optical information systems, software engineering, universal access to technology, futuristic forecasting, library consortia, vendor relations, and technology and the arts.

Every journal should have a statement along these lines, setting out the scope of the journal. Pay attention to the scope statement. When you submit articles that are clearly out of a particular journal's scope, you waste postage (or bandwidth) and look like a fool—and an awareness of foolish or arrogant behavior will usually spread beyond that journal.

Read the journal before you submit an article. Get a sense of the typical length, typical tone, and apparent audience of its articles. Setting aside the issue of formal review, what works for *ITAL* probably won't work for *Computers in Libraries*—and vice versa.

Which journals have the most prestige? I'm too biased to offer an answer. I would begin with the group of scholarly ALA divisional journals and add a few organizational, noncommercial, and commercial journals. If there is an agreed list within the profession, I don't know what it is.

Will it hurt your career to publish in secondary or tertiary journals? Probably not, unless those are your only publications. There's a cynical but generally true formulation: "Refereeing doesn't determine *whether* an article is published, only *where* it's published"—but sometimes a lesser journal is exactly the right place for a particular article.

## Journals beyond Refereed Articles

Many scholarly journals publish more than refereed articles and reviews. *Information Technology and Libraries* calls its peer-reviewed articles "feature articles," but it also publishes communications and tutorials. If something is interesting enough and within scope, *ITAL* will find a home for it.

My work has appeared fifteen times in *ITAL* and its predecessor, the *Journal of Library Automation*. At most, only one-third of those published pieces were formal refereed articles, though all of them satisfied *ITAL*'s requirements. My work has appeared many times in *Public-Access Computer Systems Review*, a refereed scholarly journal, but not one of those appearances was refereed.

Good journals, whether electronic or print, always offer clear ways to tell which articles have been refereed and which have not. My experience is that readers don't discount non-refereed articles, which must also meet the standards of the journal.

## *Pseudo-Refereed Journals*

When a journal includes the note "peer reviewed," should you assume that it follows double-blind refereeing processes? Not always, and frequently not at all. As an author or reader, you may not care—but it's worth noting the difference.

One popular web-based journal calls itself "peer reviewed." It includes the date of receipt and the date of acceptance for most articles. These dates are frequently no more than one day apart. Is it possible to get volunteer editorial board members to do two double-blind reviews, both turned around within 24 hours of the receipt of a manuscript? I suppose so—and I'm not naming the journal, giving it the benefit of the doubt—but I have my doubts.

I wrote some fifty articles for *Library Hi Tech,* which included (and may still include) the statement *"LHT* is a refereed journal" on its masthead. I served on its editorial board for fifteen years. In that time, I may have looked over half a dozen manuscripts at the editor's request, almost all of them with the author's name and affiliation intact. I can confidently assert that none of my "Common Sense Computing" articles in the journal were subjected to blind refereeing.

Should you avoid submissions to journals that don't use double-blind reviewing methods? Not at all—but as a writer or reader, it's useful to understand the distinctions.

# Tell Me Something New

In conclusion, you must have something new to offer, an addition to the literature. You must be willing to follow the forms of the journal and be a little more formal than in most other writing. You should expect more and different kinds of editorial comment than you might receive elsewhere, sometimes including suggestions for major rewrites. Do these well, and you can add top-rank journal credits to your vita.

# 4

# Report, Inform, Explain, Illuminate

**W**hen tenure and promotion are the primary motives for writing, aim for refereed articles in prestigious scholarly journals. When you have other motives, look toward a much broader range of forms and outlets. Don't ignore the journals, but think about other possibilities as well.

It's impossible to describe the world of library writing outside refereed scholarly articles in any single sensible manner. Some non-refereed journals expect scholarly or near-scholarly form, with an apparatus of footnotes and bibliography and the formal style that implies. As already noted, many refereed journals publish material other than proper scholarly articles. Then there are magazines, non-scholarly journals, newsletters, and other media. In addition to articles, you may write essays, book chapters, book reviews, and forms with no fixed name. If you have something worthwhile to say and know how to say it, the odds are you'll find a home for it.

Good library writing should report, inform, explain, or illuminate; it should argue, synthesize, reveal, or entertain. Let's consider a few areas, including those noted in chapter 1, and how you might look for places to publish.

I use the term "informal" throughout this chapter to distinguish everything that's not a refereed scholarly article. The term "non-scholarly" is demeaning and frequently wrong. "Informal" does not, of course, mean that these publications are slangy. It does mean that your own voice is likely to come through more clearly and that the range of approaches is much wider than in scholarly articles. I'll also use "article" for all of these possibilities, including book chapters, communications, and conference reports, for lack of a better inclusive term.

# What's It About?

While there's no secret formula for the ideal informal article (or at least none I've discovered), it helps to think about what you're doing before you start preparing your article.

## How You Did It Good

You may know this as the sneering catchphrase for "unworthy" journal articles. "How we did it good" is the kiss of death for serious library writing, or so I've heard.

But we learn from the experiences of others, and there's always room for enlightening reports on how you did it good—and if you're willing to write about it, we'll learn even more from how you did it bad. The latter almost never sees print, and we all understand why; honest explanations of failure are never easy.

There's little point in a straight recounting of some project unless it's an entirely new endeavor. We don't need to hear another report on the RFP process for integrated library systems or how you enlarged a library without disrupting services. Prepare a self-congratulatory set of notes for your library newsletter and let it go at that.

Interest and value come from your insights into the process, lessons learned, and experiences beyond the ordinary. You just added wireless networking throughout your library and discovered things about the disruptive effects of library stacks that you haven't seen covered in the literature? Better yet, you found ways to cope with the damping and interference? That's worth an informal article. You built your own OpenURL link resolver? That may be worth an informal article or communication. Your library and community worked with an architect to design a new library that works, using processes you haven't read about? Probably a good article topic. You studied how half a dozen libraries carried out similar projects, applied that study to your own project, and gained new insights? Tell the rest of us!

Don't assume that "how you did it good" can't make it into the premier journals. My first published article may have met review and scholarly requirements—but it was also a report on how and why we "did it good." The question is not whether an article is about how you did it good. The question is why we should care. Draw lessons from your project that speak to us, and you have a publishable article—although some critics will sneer that it's just How You Did It Good.

## Communicating Work in Progress

What if you're still working on the project? Consider whether a communication on work in progress makes sense for you and for potential readers.

This may be one of the trickiest informal article types, as you must avoid making promises that might be broken and you must also be alert to confidential situations.

When everything works, and when the lead-time of your publishing outlet is short enough, a good work-in-progress communication can be wonderful. You let the field know that something's happening while you promote the process itself and your institution's part in that process.

## Reviews and Reports

Conference reports may be a good way to break into library writing, but extended reports can also be a good way to keep things going. Thematic reports offer much more than simple "he said, she said" accountings. If you can draw conclusions about a conference or a series of programs, you add value to those programs and will probably find a ready audience.

Once you establish expertise in an area, you'll almost certainly write book reviews. There's always a need for them, and many journals have chronic shortages of good reviewers who are able to write to the required length with a short turnaround. You can go beyond simple book reviews to comparative essays, enlightening others about an aspect of the field through your informed views of related books. (See also chapter 7.)

Reviews aren't limited to books. I've done many reviews of CD-ROMs. Should you review media? Should you review related websites? Some writers have made these reviews important parts of their writing careers, establishing solid reputations based on careful, knowledgeable reviews.

## The Journalistic Approach

If you're good at finding and interviewing people, whether in person, on the phone, or via e-mail, journalistic articles may be worth considering. *American Libraries* favors journalism; so do any number of other outlets. You need a topic you care about, an approach that offers something new or different, and the right people to talk about it. Your voice may be hidden in the facts and quotations, or you may use reporting to augment your commentary.

Good journalism expands your circle of colleagues at the same time that it provides a rounded, personalized view of an issue. You need to be sure you're quoting and paraphrasing properly, that sources have appropriate institutional identification, and that what they told you was on the record. You should also be aware of any hobbyhorses your sources tend to ride. Partisans make great copy, but they don't necessarily make for the most informative articles.

I'm not very good at journalism. That's my failing. Good journalistic articles on library topics can be revealing, informative, and exciting—and when your sources aren't the same pundits everyone else quotes, such articles can also increase their visibility and serve as minor honors.

## Bringing the Outside In

Library people tend to do most of their professional reading within librarianship. That knowledge opens an opportunity that I've taken advantage of—and you can too.

Do you follow a field outside librarianship with developments that impinge on library practices? Think about the crossover and whether you should write articles that bring the outside in—that describe issues within the non-library field in ways that hold meaning for librarians.

For me, it started with the nuts and bolts of personal computing. It has extended to media technology, desktop publishing, and a growing number of other fields. For you, it could be almost anything. If you have an ongoing interest or passion, see whether there's something in it that speaks to librarians. If you're not sure, talk to your colleagues. You might be surprised. You might even gain a reputation as a guru of some sort—and should be aware that such reputations are difficult to dispel.

## Checklists and Explanations

Library publications always need good explanatory pieces, sometimes as checklists, sometimes as informal articles. New topics arise every day—OpenURL, WiFi, OAI, real-time virtual reference software support, MARC-XML crosswalks, how to define user satisfaction, statistical significance. You name it, and chances are there's a need to explain it.

My second national publication (other than a cowritten transcript from a program segment) was a checklist, "CRT Terminal Checklist," in the *Journal of Library Automation* (13:1, March 1980). I've written several explanatory articles since then. Straightforward explanations that cover new ground almost always serve readers well. Going one step further—defining a field in the course of explanation—can lead to landmark articles and awards. Explanations may not seem thrilling, but we all rely on them to stay abreast of our field. If you're good at explaining things, explanatory articles will serve your writing career and the field.

## Correlations and Consequences

The best comparative reviews draw new meaning from comparisons. Can you find correlations within the field that nobody else has noticed? Do you see consequences in a new technology or an old practice that deserve exploration? Explore those possibilities. They can move you to another level of writing—which will itself have consequences, as you become an expert, pundit, or authority.

I know of no way to show you how to find correlations, how to discover consequences. I believe that synthesis—which is an aspect of both these processes, and a laudable practice on its own—cannot be taught. How can someone show you how to add 1 + 1 + 1 to make 5? You can teach and learn analysis, but synthesis comes from within.

Your first "Aha!" moment, your first epiphany within the field, should be treasured. If you can turn that "Aha!" into a meaningful contribution to the literature, do so. We never have enough epiphanies, and most fields will always be short of natural synthesists.

Informal articles showing correlations and consequences frequently slide over into argumentation and tend toward the essay form. That's not a criticism. I draw a distinction between the argumentation in scholarly articles and the argumentation of essays. The first follows a formal structure: premise, background, methodology, evidence, conclusion. Ideally, so does informal argumentation—but essays elide some steps in order to focus on key evidence and conclusions.

# Where Should It Go?

You know what you want to say and you don't believe it makes sense as a refereed scholarly article. Where should it go, and how should you prepare it?

My first suggestion is to write where you read. Consider your favorite library publications as a possible outlet. You'll have some sense of what's expected and you'll take pride in publication. This isn't always feasible, and in some cases you'll be too nervous to try, but it's a good starting point.

If writing where you read doesn't seem to make sense, talk to your friends and acquaintances. Describe your project; ask where they think it belongs.

Then go to the publication, read a few issues, see whether the match seems reasonable.

Whether the publication is one you regularly read or one that friends have suggested, always look for author's instructions and pay attention to them. As with scholarly journals, failure to follow the rules just makes you look foolish.

If you're really not certain whether a possible article makes sense for a particular publication, ask or try. That may mean contacting an editor; it may also mean an unsolicited submission.

The worst that can happen is rejection—and if you're never rejected, you're not trying hard enough.

## Tell Me Something Good

If shorthand for scholarly articles is "tell me something new," the key for informal articles appears above, in this section's title. Tell your readers something good. Something they haven't heard before, either because of your sources, your approach, or your ability to bring in outside issues and make them real. Something that they find interesting enough to read.

You're unlikely to get as many citations for informal articles as you do for scholarly articles—but there are exceptions. You're likely to reach a broader audience and possibly inform and enlighten them more than the average scholarly article. When you hit a nerve, it's likely to be in an informal piece.

I didn't single out book chapters in this discussion. Such chapters can have the flavor of scholarly articles; they can also be formalized informal articles. Some library writers have book chapters as the heart of their publishing careers, and that's all to the good. Some book chapters are repurposed articles that have already been published—and, if you're the writer, that's even better. When you field a request for reprints, when an editor asks whether an article could appear within a collection, you know you're on your way.

Tell me something good. Enlighten me; inform me in a field I don't understand. If I understand it better after reading your article, I may remember who made that happen. Show me the consequences others have missed; put the pieces of a puzzle together, not to show off your massive brain but to help the rest of us make sense of it all.

Great informal articles cover a wide range. You can make a great writing career entirely from informal articles. We, your readers, will thank you.

# 5

## Copyright, Contracts, and Ethics

**Y**ou won't get paid for articles in most refereed journals or for most informal pieces. So why worry about copyright or contracts? I can think of two good reasons to pay attention to these issues right away:

1. When you understand the issues early on, you can establish good habits and negotiating skills that will serve you well in later years.
2. Later on, you may want to reuse your early work. If you don't make the right early decisions, this may be difficult or impossible.

I've probably been lucky in my choice of publishers, given some of the horror stories I've heard. But I've also turned down publishing agreements out of hand, in more than one case completely rewriting the proffered agreement.

The steps you take to protect your own future rights may, in some cases, complicate life for libraries and organizations that want to use your material after you've forgotten about it. I question whether this is a major issue for most library articles.

Much of this chapter boils down to three key pieces of advice:

- Don't sign a publishing agreement without reading it carefully and understanding its implications.
- Don't sign away copyright—unless there's a compelling reason to do so.
- Do learn to ask for alternative contracts and clauses; many publishers have them ready to use.

# As Soon As You Write

Copyright does not begin when you or your publisher sends two copies of a publication and a check to the Library of Congress. It doesn't begin when you print out a copy with the © symbol. Under current U.S. law and practice, expressions are protected by copyright as soon as they are put into fixed form. Technically, once it's on your hard disk, it's copyrighted.

## Copyright Basics

This is not legal advice, but the basics seem fairly clear:

> You can't copyright facts, ideas, or titles. You can only copyright *expression*—the way you've organized facts and ideas into an article or other work.

> Copyright begins at the point of fixed expression. When it ends may depend on current lawsuits and ongoing congressional action. As of this writing, corporate copyright lasts an astonishing 95 years. Personal copyright lasts an even more absurd "life of the creator plus 70 years." If the courts refuse to act, it appears probable that copyright will become essentially eternal.

> You can assign your copyright to another party—but you can also assign rights to another party without signing away copyright.

> Copyright registration primarily affects enforceability and punishment. Given the dollars involved in library writing, there's little reason for you to think about copyright registration for anything but books and other major fixed media.

# Coping with Contracts

Most book publishers and too many periodical publishers have standard contracts that assign copyright to the publisher, once you sign the contract.

Writers who care about their work should resist signing away copyright. Once you've signed over copyright your work belongs entirely to the publisher. If you wish to reuse your own work as part of a longer work or for another medium, you must request permission and may have to pay a fee.

## Work Made for Hire

When you write something as part of your job, copyright will probably belong to your library or firm. That's called "work made for hire." It's entirely honorable. The articles I write for *RLG Focus* are, presumably, work for hire, with the copyright owned by Research Libraries Group. If I was hired to consult with a group and prepared a report as part of that consultation, that report might be work for hire, depending on the terms of the contract.

When you write an article for a magazine that pays a fee, that is *not* work for hire unless you're on the magazine's staff payroll (and possibly not even then). Most of the articles I write these days earn fees. None of them are work for hire: in no case do I lose control of copyright.

If I received a publication agreement which asserted that the article was work for hire and that article hadn't been prepared on the job, there are few circumstances in which I'd accept the agreement—and the fee would have to be considerably higher than I normally see. There's nothing inherently wrong with work for hire, but "for hire" should be significant: you shouldn't lose your intellectual property rights without adequate compensation.

## First Serial Publication

If work made for hire is the worst case for your own rights, "first serial publication" or "single serial publication" may be the best case. It's also the most common case for well-managed magazines, including *American Libraries* and most of its peers.

A first serial publication agreement gives the publication exclusive rights to one and only one print version of your manuscript, limiting your ability to use it elsewhere until some specific interval after that publication. Good agreements have time limits. For example, if *American Libraries* fails to publish an article within one year of the signed agreement, it loses its exclusive right, even though it's already paid for the article.

## Online Full Text: Why Not?

Most contemporary publication agreements include an agreement that your article may appear in digital form, either on the publisher's own website or through various aggregators. If you're expecting a heresy alert here, you'll be disappointed unless you're a committed freelance writer and feel that such agreements should carry extra fees.

I believe that online full text is always a good thing for a library writer. I was delighted when *American Libraries* chose to carry "The Crawford Files" in ALOnline, its website. "Paper Persists" (published in *Online*) is one of my most-cited articles partly because *Online* posted the full text on its website.

In addition to free full text, who in the library field can object to inclusion within aggregated full-text resources? I believe in context, that an article in a print magazine carries different meanings than the same article offered as full text. But I'm also a realist: it's better for interested parties to see the article without context than to ignore it altogether.

If there's a downside to full-text availability, it is that reselling the same text—a common practice for true freelance writers—may be more difficult when the old text is readily available. For most library writers, that's not an issue. Greater visibility through full-text access can only help your reputation and writing career; I can't imagine why you'd try to prevent it.

## Secondary Rights

While "fair use" may allow educators to copy your article for classroom use, it doesn't allow anyone to incorporate your article into a published collection. That and other cases involve secondary rights—a big deal in some areas of publishing, but minor for most library writing.

Good contracts offer some leeway in handling secondary rights. You may be invited to let the publisher handle secondary rights in exchange for 50 percent of the receipts; after all, most people looking to reuse material will go to the publisher first. You can sometimes opt to reject such reuse, insisting that all requests come directly to you. Some publishers won't handle secondary rights at all; some extend fair use as a matter of practice; some presume that they control secondary rights.

When offered the choice, I've allowed the publisher to handle secondary rights—except for my own right to reuse the material. I've probably received less than $500 total in secondary rights during my entire writing career, and that's more than I expected. In each case of contractual reuse, doing it myself would have been a waste of time and energy. If you believe your journal or magazine article would make a good movie, you should think about secondary rights more carefully, but that's not an issue for most library publications.

## Modifying the Boilerplate

You're looking at the publishing agreement and you don't like what you read. Not only does the agreement lack choices, it seems to favor the publisher at your expense. What should you do?

1. First, ask the publisher for its alternative agreement, the one that leaves more rights in your name. For a time, even *Information Technology and*

*Libraries* had two different agreements, with the more author-friendly one produced upon request.

2. If that doesn't work, point out clauses that bother you and suggest alternative language. I rewrote an entire agreement in one case, removing the language that I considered unfair. The publisher accepted the rewritten agreement without further discussion. You may not be so lucky.

3. When a publisher insists that its unbalanced contract is the only way it works, you have a tough decision. Do you want to encourage such unfair behavior? Is there another, more writer-friendly, outlet for your article? Or is this a case where you hold your nose and sign away your rights? I've done that—and, although money has never been the issue in such cases, I've always regretted it. At that point, ethical issues come into play.

4. The least fair agreements I've dealt with have come from publishers that either don't pay at all or pay trivial sums a few months after publication. The fairest agreements have come from publishers that pay acceptably well, on acceptance. Draw your own conclusions.

If this sounds complicated and abstruse, some of it is. You'll relearn careful reading and the art of negotiation. Be aware that article contracts are trivial compared to book contracts, which go on for pages and almost always involve negotiation.

You say you don't want copyright protection for life plus 70 years? You'd like to have a clear way to make your work available after a reasonable time, without opening it to unreasonable use? Help may be at hand.

Lawrence Lessig and a group of colleagues have formed Creative Commons (www.creativecommons.org), a nonprofit "intellectual property conservancy to help artists, writers, musicians and scientists share their intellectual works with the public on generous terms." At this writing, Creative Commons is still being formed. By the time you read this, it may offer ways for you to register works as available under appropriate circumstances. There are other ways to cope with copyright, such as "copyleft" licenses and explicit limitation of claimed copyright.

Don't sign away your rights accidentally—but think carefully about when it makes sense to waive some of those rights deliberately. You count on others for inspiration; can reuse of your words carry that process along for the future?

## Ethical Considerations

When should you walk away from a publication or publisher, or avoid writing for it in the first place? How should you handle ideas inspired by others?

Ethical issues (beyond straightforward plagiarism and theft) tend to be personal and complex. A number of situations may bother you. Whenever a situation strikes you as bothersome, there may (or may not) be an ethical issue.

Only you can determine the point at which you move from being bothered to regarding a situation as unethical. I'll raise a few cases where ethical issues *might* come into play.

## Publishers and Publications

Which of these cases would cause you to avoid a publisher or publication?

1. You've been writing articles for Publication X, which charges subscription prices you regard as high but not unreasonable. A new publisher buys X and immediately doubles or triples the price, to a level that you consider unreasonably high for the publication.

2. Publisher A suggests that you write a book on topic Y when you're aware that a similar book was just published (or is about to be published) by Publisher B. Looking at A's list of publications, you find an uncanny resemblance to the topical coverage of B, suggesting a pattern of "fighting titles."

3. To make things more complicated, you wrote the book on Y for Publisher B, and Publisher A's proposed contract is good enough to outweigh any possible loss in royalties from Publisher B.

4. A colleague has been writing a column for Magazine W, and told you that she was getting $400 per issue. An editor from Magazine W approaches you suggesting that you could take over the column for $350 an issue, although you know the colleague wasn't planning to stop.

5. Publisher C wants to publish your book and offers a good advance and a reasonable royalty rate—but the contract includes a clause that gives Publisher C the right of first refusal to your next book in the library field, and the publisher won't negotiate that clause.

6. Magazine V is ready to use and pay for your article that was published six months ago in Magazine U, word for word, as long as you make up a new title—and Magazine V won't include a credit line for the original publication.

What would you do? These are six examples that require some thought; the list could go on for pages. These aren't all straw men, although at least one of them may be entirely mythical. I've faced two of the six cases, and made what I now consider to be the wrong choice both times. One or two of the situations may not strike experienced writers as being bothersome in any way; after all, ethics are largely personal.

## Colleagues and Concepts

You can't copyright ideas, just as you can't copyright facts. The law may be clear on this point; ethical considerations can be more difficult. A few examples:

1. A colleague mentions a novel idea that you haven't seen in the literature. You know the colleague might write a piece about the idea, but you also know you're likely to write it up faster and better. Should you do so—without checking with the colleague first? Does it make a difference where you heard the idea (e.g., in a bar, over dinner, in an ALA discussion group, during a committee meeting)?

2. You hear a presentation at a conference taken from work in progress that gives you a great idea for an article or book. The facts presented are in that handy set of PowerPoint printouts. Are you free to use the facts and ideas without attribution? Are you free to do so *with* attribution, even though you know you'll publish before the work is complete and the researchers have a chance to publish?

3. Reading a scholarly article in Journal D, you realize that you could turn it into a publishable popular article for Magazine T, taking the ideas and organization but substituting your own wording. Is this appropriate with attribution? Without attribution? If you're fairly sure that the writer of the article will read Magazine T, does that change the situation?

You get the idea—and, again, there are many similar situations to consider. These aren't easy issues. The first consideration for such ethical questions is a traditional one that goes by different names in many religions and philosophies. Paraphrased for this discussion, it reads: How would you wish to be treated in such circumstances—if you had the idea, made the presentation, or wrote the scholarly article?

It all ties together. Appropriate copyright law (which is not necessarily what we have in the United States today) helps to ensure appropriate balances among writers, intermediaries, and readers. Good contracts should represent ethical documents, spelling out fair arrangements between the parties. Beyond copyright and contract, ethical sensitivity in your writing and publishing will (I believe) help you in the long run.

# 6

## Working with Editors

**E**very prose writer in every field, at every stage of their career, can benefit from judicious editing. That's my belief and that belief guides most of this chapter.

If you believe otherwise—if your words are so golden that any modifications can only do harm—you probably think the title of this chapter should be "battling with editors." You're setting yourself up for a career full of struggle and are almost certainly valuing your work a little too highly.

So far, we've discussed aspects of getting started: why you want to write, a few notes on mechanics, two primary approaches to traditional library publishing, and the need to consider copyright, contracts, and ethics. This and the next few chapters deal with building a path, establishing yourself as a writer.

"Building a path" may suggest something far more deliberate than makes sense for most of us. I do not suggest that you fire up Microsoft Project and establish a set of milestones in your writing career, although I'm sure some library writers have planned their progress almost that formally. I'm not one of them, and it's the accidental aspects of my writing and speaking that have made it interesting. If you're lucky and open to new possibilities, that's likely to be true for you as well.

In the next few chapters, I'll discuss some aspects of writing in the twenty-first century that may not involve having someone else edit your writing. But first it makes sense to discuss working with an editor.

# Golden Words

How dare that stupid editor suggest changes in my plangent prose? If she's such a great writer, where's her list of publications? I know more about writing than he'll ever learn; I refuse to let my perfect prose be damaged by his need to feel important. My words are golden; leave them alone.

I suspect every editor, whether amateur or professional, has picked up these messages either directly or indirectly. I've heard too many part-time writers moan and groan about editors who have ruined their submissions not to recognize a pattern. It's easy to pile on the editor, particularly when you have a more impressive publication record.

It's also generally wrong, and is harmful to both your ability to improve your writing and the likelihood that editors will want to deal with you. To restate the opening of this chapter: I do not believe there is any writer in any field whose prose can't be improved by judicious editing. Period.

Which is not to say that all editors know what they're doing, that you should blindly accept every editorial suggestion, or that an editor won't screw up your work at some point. They don't, you shouldn't, they will.

On the whole, most editors do the best they can—and that's frequently very good indeed. If there's one aspect of being an established writer that troubles me, it's that too many editors are reluctant to tear into my manuscripts with gleeful intent to find what's wrong and suggest improvements.

## Amateur Hour

When you submit articles to a refereed scholarly journal, a newsletter, or most secondary library periodicals, you're probably dealing with a volunteer editorial staff. In other words, amateurs—people whose primary job is something other than editing—are editing you.

That's true for *Information Technology and Libraries*. It's true for most other ALA divisional publications and quite a few other journals. In some cases, you'll have a combination of amateur editor and professional or contract managing or copy editors—but there's also the chance that those copy editors don't understand the field as well as you and your editor.

When you submit an article to a refereed journal, you gain an additional level of editing—the reviewers. They don't know who you are, but they do know what bothers them about your paper. Take their comments seriously. If you're lucky enough to get specific editorial comments, consider them. Are you sure you made that point clearly? Is it possible that this paragraph really is redundant or conflicts with an earlier sentence?

When you submit a revised draft, your work isn't done. That draft will probably go through at least one round of copyediting, with an emphasis on correct style and clarity. In many cases, you will get one more look at your manuscript: the "galley" stage.

## Editing and Writing Are Different Skills

What about the professional (or amateur) editor whose publication record doesn't begin to match your own? Maybe the heading above is all the answer you need. Most editors also write, but editing is a different skill—and a mediocre writer may be a first-rate editor.

Assume that editorial suggestions are made in good faith. Think about them seriously. They may not all be right, but they're typically based on experience and thought. If an editorial suggestion strikes you as egregiously wrongheaded, consider the reasons for the suggestion. Is that section of your manuscript muddled or arcane enough to mislead the editor? Editors are almost always intelligent readers; if they have trouble making sense of your writing, what does that say about your success with your intended readership?

## Reading the Galleys

Frequently, your only chance to deal with editorial changes comes in the form of "galleys"—a traditional term for sheets pulled from hand-inked type, which currently represents edited pages that may not include final pagination and other procedures.

Those galleys are likely to come with warnings that you can only correct errors, that it's too expensive to rewrite at this point. In terms of typesetting expense, that's probably nonsense. Almost nothing gets typeset anymore. Your galleys represent word-processing or desktop-publishing output, and changing even a paragraph costs no more than retyping that paragraph.

It's a convenient form of nonsense, one that protects writer and editor alike. On the editor's side, it's critical to wind down the production process, and pagination may have already begun based on the galley stage. On the writer's side, you want to see your work in print; you should make reasonable compromises to get it there.

I adopted an accidental approach to reading galleys that has always worked well. I don't compare them with the original manuscript unless something seems terribly wrong. I read the galleys carefully, word by word, sentence by sentence, but within their own context. Normally, I never go back to my original manuscript. My guess is that this practice will save you needless grief and help you to move from "golden words" to clearer writing.

There's a danger here, of course. Maybe you crafted a killer phrase or paragraph that was damaged by some editorial intern or a staffer who was in a hurry or had a really bad night. If the prose was that special, you probably have it in the back of your mind and will wonder where it went.

More likely, the editor will make appropriate decisions that differ slightly from your original writing. If the editing is sensitive—if they haven't rewritten your words in their style—such changes will go right past you when you read the galleys. In my experience, that's a good thing. Why argue over changes that don't bother you as a reader?

### Blind Faith

Many magazines and newsletters don't provide galleys for author review. *American Libraries* is one of those. They've already paid for your article (*American Libraries* pays for articles on acceptance), they have first-rate editors who also write articles, and they trust their own judgment. They may inquire if something strikes them as peculiar, but usually you won't see changes until the article appears in print. Some magazines also rewrite extensively to suit a house style while retaining the best of your prose.

Welcome to the real world.

I'm not sure what else to say. If *American Libraries'* editors were less skillful, I'd talk about their cavalier attitude—but, with one or two tiny exceptions, these editors have always improved my writing. I would say the same for my editors at *EContent* and *Online* (both of which do send galleys), but their editing has been so skillful that it's transparent—until I do go back to the original and see a problem they've solved.

Other publications with inferior editing staff may also take what you send and turn it into what they want. In most cases, your best recourse is to stop dealing with that publication—and if it's egregious, send them a letter nailing the problem and saying what you intended to say.

## Sometimes They're Wrong

Editors make mistakes. I've had to undo changes in half a dozen edited manuscripts. At least one professionally edited article has appeared with a mistake I would never have made—but one that was easy for an editor to make.

My own experience has been worst with freelance book copy editors who didn't understand the library field. That's a specialized problem, one you shouldn't encounter until you work on a book. Copyediting changes in book manuscripts are almost always suggestions. If you don't agree, don't make the changes.

If an editor suggests or makes a change that causes an error, just correct it—and it doesn't hurt to admit that your own prose may have been ambiguous.

If an editor suggests a change that confounds your intent or weakens your prose, you might object, but think about it first. You might even show the original and suggested changes to colleagues. Is the original really better? Do you have friends who will criticize your golden words?

Be blunt when you need to be, preferably within a polite envelope. Calling someone to accuse them of a deliberate hatchet job may be counterproductive; sending a memo suggesting that there may have been a misunderstanding is likely to yield better results.

You will probably see some printed publications that you feel are inferior to your drafts. If the inferiority damages your meaning, feel free to send a letter for publication and add the publication to your informal blacklist. That's likely to be rare. Most of the time, "wrong" is a value judgment. Unless your first Pulitzer or Nobel Prize is sitting on your mantel, consider the possibility that the editor may be right.

# Waiting and Rejection

Editors don't just revise your work, and the editor of a major publication probably won't be the one who does that revision. Editors also deal with the most frustrating aspect of writing for publication: waiting for acceptance and dealing with rejection.

How long should you wait for an editor to accept or reject a submission? What should you do with rejected manuscripts? There's no simple answer for either question, except to note that the first question may become less interesting as you grow into a writing career and establish working relationships with editors you trust.

## The Waiting Game

Some publications include typical review periods in writers' guidelines. Unfortunately, many don't—and those that do can't always meet their own guidelines. If guidelines do appear, you should note them and add enough time for mail delays. If, for example, the guidelines say that submissions should be responded to within four to six weeks, I'd probably wait seven or eight weeks. At that point, it's entirely appropriate to send an inquiry letter or e-mail. If there's no response, a phone call may be your next step. If that doesn't work, your best bet may be to send a formal withdrawal notice—"I'm withdrawing this submission"—and try elsewhere.

Some writers try to shortcut that process through simultaneous submission, sending the same article to more than one publication and going with the first acceptance. That's a dangerous game, particularly in a field as small as library publishing. Assume that editors for rival publications do communicate, particularly since library publications are rarely in direct competition with one another. Many publications explicitly disallow multiple submission in their formal guidelines; I am not aware of any library publication that welcomes such submissions. What happens when two editors both accept your article simultaneously? For that matter, what if Magazine Z accepts the article after two weeks—and Magazine Y, with a stated four-week review period, is ready to accept it a week later? In the short run, you have a contract. In the long run, your chances at Magazine Y will probably suffer.

You are not obliged to sit and wait indefinitely. If you feel that the stated guidelines are too long for a particular article, say so along with your submission. "I'd love to have Magazine X publish this, but I really need a response within a month given the timely nature of the article." Phrased politely, such a note shouldn't damage your chances, unless you habitually request an unreasonably short turnaround.

What to do if there are no turnaround times in the writers' guidelines? If possible, ask around. Do you know anyone at the publication or who has written for them before? Does a friend of a friend know the editor well enough to make a casual inquiry?

If you're an established writer or well known in your field, you can probably initiate the inquiry yourself. A quick note to the editor before submission may be enough—"I have an article I think you'd like. Roughly how long could I expect to wait for a response?" That's not really an unreasonable question even if this is your first time out. If the answer is "There's no way of knowing," consider how anxious you really are to deal with this publication.

Books are more difficult, typically involving longer review periods—but you will almost never submit a book in its entirety until a contract has been signed. (See chapter 13 for more discussion of books.) Scholarly journals also tend to involve longer review periods because referees are involved. It can easily take months for a journal to respond.

You need to establish your own limits for dealing with sticky situations. What do you do when a response seems late and your inquiry draws the reply that the editors need to think about it for a few more weeks? What do you do when a publication's editors are consistently late in responding, later than you consider appropriate? I would probably stop working with the latter publication (but might discuss the problem with them first); you may be more patient.

## Dealing with Rejection

Your work will be rejected at times. That's not universally true, but if you never face rejection it may mean you're not pushing your own boundaries enough. What do you do when an article is rejected?

Consider the nature of the rejection. If a magazine editor says that an article doesn't meet the magazine's current needs, that doesn't mean the article is no good—particularly if the editor goes on to say, "We published an article on that topic too recently." Try elsewhere, reworking the article if necessary to suit another magazine or journal. I've published articles in *Online* based on rejected submissions to *American Libraries*—and vice versa. If the article bounces more than two or three times, take a hard look at your work; maybe the article isn't ready for publication.

Was the article really within the publication's scope? Go back to the guidelines and to recent issues of the magazine or journal. If you write a superb 5,000-word treatise on the relationship between academic portals and library services (studded with documented facts and footnotes) and submit it to *American Libraries,* you're nearly assured of a rejection, both because of length and approach. *College & Research Libraries,* on the other hand, might be delighted with the article, as might several other publications.

Don't give up on an article you're sure is worthwhile, but don't set your heart on getting every article published. Some articles just don't fit anywhere.

It may pay to give up on certain editors or publications. If you've submitted several pieces that you believe are in scope, follow guidelines, and would work well within the publication—and they've all been rejected—try to find out why. Does the editor dislike you personally? Are you associated too heavily with a different publication? Is there something about your style that just grates on the editor? If so—well, there are always other publications.

# 7

# Reviewing

**W**riting in any professional field can involve more than just writing articles, particularly when you wish to establish yourself in the field. This chapter and the next cover three of the primary ways you can (and probably should) contribute to library literature after your first couple of articles and as you're building a path. In the case of reviewing, you can start before your first article and may find that reviewing is your favorite form of writing.

You can think of this area as giving back to the profession, but that may be ingenuous. Book reviews make as much sense on your curriculum vitae as most other publications. Editorial board service is as honorable as any other committee service. Editing a significant publication may count for more than most writing. Reviewing, working on an editorial board, and editing all involve you with writers and exercise your literary muscles, but in different ways than pure writing.

A caveat is in order. Most of this book draws heavily from personal experience. This chapter doesn't. I wrote my first published book review shortly after writing my second serious article. It was an atypical feature review comparing two books. I've written fewer than a dozen book reviews in all, and not a single book review in at least five years.

I'm not a "regular," and I'm no expert on what it takes to become a recognized reviewer. I don't believe I could write a review to the length limits of *Library Journal,* and I regard that as a personal weakness. I have much more experience reviewing CD-ROMs, as noted later in this chapter. But the brevity and vagueness of this chapter represent reality: I don't know enough to offer a comprehensive discussion.

# Writing Book Reviews

The library field always needs good book reviewers and, these days, thought-ful reviewers for nonprint materials and websites as well. A book review is a mini-article that follows its own special rules. A comparative book review may become a full-length article.

You need four primary qualifications to work effectively as a book reviewer:

1. *Good reading and writing skills.* You need to read critically and write in a coherent, understandable manner.
2. *Expertise within a subfield.* You must have a basis for judging a work or website. That doesn't mean being the world's foremost authority on the area; it does mean understanding it well enough to provide back-ground for your review judgments.
3. *Writing to length.* While some book review columns can handle extended essays, most publications establish fairly rigid length limita-tions for reviews. If you can't properly describe and judge a book in less than 1,000 words and your editor will only accept 350, you're in trouble.
4. *Meeting deadlines.* When you're offered a book to review, the offer fre-quently comes with a deadline. You must be able to read the book, check related works, and prepare your review within the allotted time. This is good practice, as you'll find yourself meeting deadlines as your writing career flourishes.

Many professional journals and library magazines continually invite potential reviewers; some occasionally publish notices that they're looking for new reviewers. With smaller journals, it doesn't take much to move from reviewer to review editor. In both positions, you need to show expertise, spe-cialized writing capability, and the ability to meet deadlines.

## Over the Transom

With rare exceptions, book reviewing is always commissioned. People don't read interesting books, then send reviews to *Library Journal* over the transom (without prior contact) in the hope they'll be published. That wouldn't work at all for early review media (such as *Library Journal*), where reviews ideally appear within a few weeks or months of publication and are used as selection tools in libraries.

Publications that carry large numbers of book reviews build and maintain pools of reviewers, soliciting new participants as needed. When you apply for inclusion within the pool, you'll probably be asked to submit a few sample reviews—or better yet, to include copies of published reviews. If accepted, you'll be added to the list as a specialist in certain areas, then sent books (or bound galleys) within those areas to review. The publication establishes length limits, deadlines, and reward structures, which may include modest payment as well as copies of the books themselves.

Other publications use a variety of means to solicit reviews. A book review editor may establish a contact list, then ask one specific person who's likely to be suitable or ask for volunteers from the list. You may be contacted by an editor you've never met, for a publication you've never submitted to, with an invitation to review a specific book based on the editor's awareness of your expertise and track record.

## Benefits and Problems

Most of the time, for most library publications, you see three benefits from writing book reviews:

1. Your writing gets published in a form that's widely read by other librarians.
2. Your review helps librarians and others to make wise decisions.
3. You get free books.

If you get paid, so much the better. If you continue to review within a specific field, you may find yourself invited to write feature reviews, articles in the field, even give speeches in the field.

The biggest problems for most reviewers have already been mentioned. It's tough to summarize a book and offer a useful judgment in one or two brief paragraphs. If you're not sufficiently familiar with the related literature, your review may be misleading. If you're pressed for time, you may be tempted to skim the book instead of reading it carefully, and that can lead to misleading or erroneous reviews.

And, of course, you can make enemies. If you write nothing but positive reviews, either you lead a charmed life or you're not an effective reviewer. What happens when you write a negative review and later meet the writer— or worse, when you agree to review a book by someone you know and find that it's not very good? Some writers divorce themselves from books once they're written, but for many of us a book remains a part of us. It's hard to cope with sharply negative comments on our printed-and-bound children.

## Problematic Reviewing

As an author, you must be willing to read negative reviews of your work without defensiveness or an urge to reply or attack the reviewer. Even if you feel the review is fundamentally wrong, it's generally a bad idea to respond; it's a fight you probably can't win.

There's a difference between negative reviews and problematic reviews. I avoid one kind of problematic review by turning down invitations to review books by close friends and acquaintances—but also by rejecting opportunities to review books by people I dislike. I don't necessarily suggest that you do the same—after all, some of us make thousands of acquaintances and such scrupulousness could eliminate most possible reviewers. But such reviews always raise potential difficulties. Will you be too easy on a book because you like the author? When you dislike the author, are you really reviewing the book—or are you taking the opportunity to put down the author?

In my own experience as a reviewee and in talking to other authors, I've seen a few specific problematic cases:

Reviews that attack the book as a surrogate for the author, or that attack a coauthored book or a collection based on animus toward a single author.

Reviews that show clear evidence of skimming rather than reading.

Reviews of American library books in some other countries that dwell on the lack of international coverage in the book. That's entirely appropriate if the book claims universality and is worth mentioning in all cases, but it's a little unreasonable to attack a book for something it never claimed to do.

Reviews that push the reviewer's agenda at the expense of the writer's intent.

Reviews that attack the book because it's not some other book that the reviewer wanted to read. To give an example, at least one reviewer of my book *Current Technologies in the Library: An Informal Overview* was outraged because I didn't concentrate on *future* technological possibilities, and particularly because, in the high-tech world of 1988, I began with "the printed page" as the most important current technology in libraries.

I suspect that the last case is quite common. It's also entirely understandable. You know there's a gap in the field. You agree to review a book that could fill that gap, even though the title and introductory chapters suggest that it has a different purpose. It's only human nature to be disappointed that the book wasn't what you hoped it would be. It's also wrong, at least in my opinion. It's unfair to the writer and to possible readers to review the book you *hoped* to read if the writer is clear about his or her actual intent. You can, of course, express your disappointment that the book didn't go in another direction; that may even encourage the writer (or some other writer) to fill the perceived gap.

## Nonprint Reviewing

Most book reviews spend no time at all on the physical quality of the book—the ink used, the paper, the binding (unless there's a problem), or the layout and typography for primarily textual books. Readers assume a table of contents, page numbers, running heads, readable typefaces, and appropriate back matter for nonfiction books (index, bibliography if needed, etc.) and will only comment when these standard parts of books are missing. Books are, after all, highly evolved technological devices representing centuries of improvement and common understanding of the norms.

I reviewed scores of CD-ROMs during the few years when "title" CD-ROMs (as opposed to databases, games, pornography, and educational tools) flourished. As with websites and other nonprint media, the norms are not as well established. I found it necessary to build a scorecard approach for each CD-ROM, noting various aspects of how it worked and was organized as well as the content itself. The scorecard added a questionable sense of objectivity to the subjective review, but it also helped ensure that I actually checked issues of readability, performance, installation, and the like.

Who worries about installing a book? You open it and start reading. If the book is three or ten years old, you still open it and start reading. But a four-year-old CD-ROM, or a website optimized for a particular browser or screen size, is a different animal entirely; it may not work at all for the reviewer.

Does that make reviewing nonprint media more difficult than reviewing books? Not really; it just calls for different approaches and raises different issues. You typically don't need as much grounding in comparative resources to review a CD-ROM, for example; there aren't likely to be four works comparable to *Totally Mad* or *Total Joplin*. You do need to establish which aspects of the work should be reviewed for a given publication and the basis for judging the work. This is most obvious with media such as movies on DVD, where it may be entirely appropriate to give a rave review to a movie that you consider trash, because the DVD presents the trash so admirably.

One piece of advice that works for all writing may be most critical for reviewing, and particularly nonprint reviewing. Read the publication you plan to write for. Become familiar with its needs and practices. If you're not clear about expectations, ask.

And if you believe that a potential review poses serious problems for you, decline the opportunity. Even as part of a reviewing pool, you should always be able to say, "I just can't do this one," particularly when there are good reasons. Say so right away, so the editor can find another reviewer. You'll have other chances if you want them.

# 8

## Editorial Boards and Editing

**M**any professional journals, newsletters, and magazines rely on volunteer editors. Most of these publications—and many that use professional editors—also have editorial boards. Some journals draw most or all of their manuscript reviewers from their editorial boards.

Editorial board service can be a gentle way to support your field, with the level of effort varying enormously. Editing can be much more laborious but also more rewarding.

### Editorial Boards

Describing a standard editorial board is like describing a standard library periodical. I can't think of a better way to suggest the range of editorial board experience than to recount my own four experiences serving on boards. Each has been distinctive—so distinctive that I can't say whether these models reflect the full range of what you'll find.

Some members of editorial boards are appointed for limited terms. Some are invited by editors or publishers and their terms can involve lengthy service, ending when you resign or the editor asks you to leave. If you feel you'd be an addition to an editorial board, get in touch with the editor and ask how it works. You'd never ask to serve on an editorial board for a publication you don't already read and enjoy, would you?

Three aspects have been true of all the editorial boards I've served on, and I suspect they're fairly standard:

1. Payment has never consisted of anything more than a free subscription to the journal or magazine, refreshments or meals during editorial board meetings, and recognition through listing on the publication's masthead. Some commercial publications may pay editorial board members, but I haven't encountered them.

2. Every editorial board has been, at least in part, an acquisitions board—that is, editorial board members are encouraged to find good authors and articles.

3. Editorial board service has always been a great way to meet people and stay in touch with current issues in the field. Each board has been a pleasure.

## Library Hi Tech *(Journal and Newsletter)*

Beginning in 1986 and continuing until 2000, I served on the *Library Hi Tech* editorial board. During the early years, this had two essential aspects:

1. Appearing on the journal's masthead, to the presumed mutual benefit of the journal's reputation and one's own.

2. Attending two editorial breakfasts each year, one at the ALA Annual Conference and one at the ALA Midwinter Meeting, where a remarkable cross-section of people within the field got together to discuss trends, make suggestions about the journal, and get to know each other. You'd be surprised at the big names who showed up in the Pierian Press suite at 6:30 a.m. and stayed until 10 a.m. or later, fueled by coffee, juice, and pastries and offering wildly varied but well-informed perspectives on the state of the field.

Later, breakfast attendance grew sparse and the journal reduced the size of its editorial board. A new publisher turned the breakfasts into restaurant meals with formal agendas, still offering the chance to debate the state of the journal and the state of the field.

Once in a while, the editor might ask me to evaluate a paper, typically with the author's name present and the review handled less formally than proper refereeing. Frequently, board members would be asked to suggest topics for theme issues—and whether we'd consider editing (and acquiring papers for) those issues.

## Information Technology and Libraries

In 1986 I also began to attend *Information Technology and Libraries* editorial board meetings—first as informal liaison from the *LITA Newsletter,* later

(1988–94) as an ex officio member as *LITA Newsletter* editor, and twice since then as an appointed member of the board (1994–95 and 1999–2002).

*ITAL* board members serve as referees. That's essential, and I'd expect the same to be true of any editorial board for a refereed scholarly journal. Sometimes the editor sends out a paper title and asks for two qualified (and interested) reviewers; sometimes you just get the paper with a deadline and set of expectations.

If you can't meet deadlines, you have no business serving on an editorial board that includes referee duties. If you're uncomfortable judging other writers' work, which means rejecting it more than half of the time for many journals, you should stay away from this sort of editorial board.

Refereeing is never the whole story. The editorial board also advises the editor, discusses problems of copy flow, suggests special themes, looks for good writers, and may even pore over statistical analyses of reader surveys.

For an ALA divisional journal, you must be a division member to serve on the board, so a free subscription would be superfluous. Some editorial boards have refreshments at their meetings; some don't. Compensation consists of a valuable item in your vita, meeting people in the field (some of whom can help your own career), and playing a vital part in keeping professional journals healthy.

## Public-Access Computer Systems Review

*The PACS Review* was an early electronic journal, started years before it could appear on the Web. The journal began as an offshoot of PACS-L, the Public-Access Computer Systems List, founded by Charles W. Bailey Jr. at the University of Houston. I joined the *PACS Review* editorial board shortly after it began in 1989, and remained on the board until the journal was formally dissolved in 2000.

In many ways the *PACS Review* board was comparable to the *ITAL* board, except that there was no term limit (because there was no parent body) and no formal face-to-face meetings. It was an electronic journal. All "meetings" were held on a closed list. But editorial board members reviewed submissions for the refereed portion of the journal, advised on editorial policy, looked for new writers—and, early on, pursued an extended discussion on the advisability of publishing an annual print version.

Many electronic journals have emerged since the *PACS Review*. While some have died, others survive—though few have had such long, distinguished, and influential publication records as the *PACS Review*. I don't believe you can damage your reputation by serving on the editorial board of a fledgling e-journal if you have the opportunity, time, and determination. At worst it will fail. At best, you'll be a founding part of a new force in library journalism. No pay, no free breakfasts, and there's no paid subscription to waive on your behalf—but the best e-journals can be as important as the best print journals.

## Online *Magazine*

This editorial board was an odd one, of a sort you may encounter as well. I served on it from 1991 through 1997, at which point the editor and publisher decided that the editorial board no longer served any real purpose. *Online* is a magazine, not a journal; that eliminates peer review as a board service. During my seven years on the board, I found few expectations other than answering occasional questions about the magazine and keeping an eye out for promising writers.

Did having an editorial board add credibility to *Online*'s masthead? Probably not. *Online* established credibility through its articles and consistent editorial quality. The editorial board was eventually found to be extraneous.

# Editing

What does it mean to be an editor?

On the volunteer side of library publishing, that depends almost entirely on the publication. For journals, the editor's job typically includes finding writers, encouraging those writers, assigning articles to reviewers, and making sure the whole process results in a timely, worthwhile publication. Meanwhile, a managing editor or professional staff handle most or all of the manuscript editing.

For newsletters, the editor's job may involve manuscript editing along with finding writers and making sure deadlines are observed. It may also include layout and copy fitting.

Good editing may be more difficult than good writing. Poor editorial work can damage a publication, while poor writing mostly means the writer won't be published in better publications.

A successful term as editor of a high-profile publication looks great on your vita and can do wonders for your reputation and circle of acquaintances. But don't apply for editorial positions unless you're fairly sure you have the time, diligence, and skills to do them well.

I've never served as editor for a journal. That's by choice and reflects laziness and a dislike for approaching and hounding would-be writers. I've seen what good journal editors do and have the greatest respect for that task—which is why I've avoided doing it myself.

## Newsletter Editing

If you want to pursue editing, you might consider starting at the local newsletter level or as a guest editor in a state or national publication. Guest-editing a theme issue exposes you to the need to find authors and encourage (or nag) them to meet deadlines; make sure that a set of manuscripts works together well; see to it that manuscripts are revised as needed; and, typically, prepare an editorial to finish off the process.

Things can go wrong, and when you operate on the edge, things go wrong more frequently. If you can't handle the strain of being short two articles when the publication cycle requires manuscripts a week from now, and you didn't realize the benefits of having extra writers in reserve, you may not be a good candidate for journal or newsletter editing.

Newsletter editing can include finding writers and meeting deadlines. You'll probably also revise manuscripts and organize issues as a whole. You may be able to shift the course of a publication, and might do your own layout and copy fitting.

I've had two overlapping experiences as a newsletter editor, both of which were edifying and good uses of my time. I served as the founding editor of *Information Standards Quarterly* and designed that newsletter in cooperation with others. In the case of the *LITA Newsletter,* thanks to organizational changes, I was able to transform an existing newsletter—a process that was, unfortunately, reversed years later. I don't suggest that either of these are typical cases, but I've seen several instances where a new editor has had profound effects on a newsletter.

There's not much to say about my experiences with the *Information Standards Quarterly,* and most of that might not be applicable. It's not often that you'll be the founding editor of a publication (unless it's your own idea), and the fixed requirements of a standards organization determined most of what I did in that position. The *LITA Newsletter* is another story.

## LITA Newsletter

My oddest claim to fame may be that I edited more than half the print issues of the *LITA Newsletter.* It's a claim I wish was not true. I inherited the newslet-

ter from Carol Parkhurst, who did a first-rate job of making the most of limited space and flexibility. As a typeset publication handled through the ALA's
publishing services, the *LITA Newsletter* had a small page budget (eight pages
three times a year, twelve pages for the post-Annual Conference issue) and a
difficult set of deadlines. Most of the copy was filtered through three section
editors, who provided single reports in generally neutral voices. A few columns
offered more distinctive writing, as did the necessarily brief program reports.

The Library and Information Technology Association (LITA) had just
reorganized when I took over in 1985, eliminating sections in the process. I
scrambled for "topical editors" early on with little success, then found that
longer, signed, program and interest group reports, lightly edited to retain the
voice of the writer, were better uses of space. But there wasn't enough space.

That was when desktop publishing on a budget became plausible. I
talked the board into letting me convert the *LITA Newsletter* to desktop form
and use the savings to publish more pages. While my amateur status and
early printer limitations meant that the next two years' issues were crudely
formatted, I was able to run more and better program and discussion reports.
The next year the newsletter had four 16-page issues; the year after that, two
16- and two 24-page issues; later years saw even larger issues with more
extensive reporting, including one 48-page issue and a one-time 122-page
paperback yearbook.

I learned three key lessons in building the *LITA Newsletter,* two of them
applicable to many editing situations:

1. If you're frustrated by too few pages, look closely at the budget and see
   what flexibility there might be.
2. Edit carefully—but retain the writer's voice. A 48-page newsletter in
   one neutral tone is far too long. The same newsletter with more than
   thirty bylined contributions, each with its own voice, may not be long
   enough.
3. When you make an inviting home for informal contributions such as
   program and discussion group reports, it's easier to find writers. After
   my second year, I never found it necessary to personally recruit
   reporters; one call for contributors and a couple of broadcast e-mails
   did it all.

## Other Editorial Possibilities

If you're interested in editing but nervous about taking on such a task, there
may be intermediate possibilities. Many publications have separate book

review editors. *Information Technology and Libraries* has a software review editor. In both cases, while the editor may also write some of the reviews, the primary mix of duties is similar to that of a journal editor but on a smaller scale and with better-defined outcomes.

Some publications have column and section editors, people who take responsibility to fill a specific slot in the publication but not necessarily to write the content.

As noted earlier, there's also guest editing; this is comparable to journal editing but is limited to one issue or a cluster of related articles. Guest editing may be the best way to see whether you can handle full-scale editing, since it involves most aspects of editing. There's one key difference: when you edit a single issue, you're finished. When you edit a publication, you always have the next set of deadlines to deal with.

If there's a downside to editing (other than pressure), it's the odd effect it has on your writing career. Specifically, you probably won't run articles by yourself (other than editorial columns and conference reports) in your own publication. The conflicts inherent in doing this are so substantial that it's easiest to avoid them entirely. That means, of course, that if you have great articles to contribute in your specific field, you're likely to contribute them to a different and possibly rival publication. That's also a tough call. Fortunately, most volunteer editor positions have limited terms; after you're done, you can go back to submitting articles wherever they work best.

# 9

# Nontraditional Writing
## *Discussion Lists and Weblogs*

The backbone of most writing careers may be articles and books, but for more than a decade there have been nontraditional routes as well. This chapter and the next consider nontraditional writing using the Internet and World Wide Web as carriers. Both chapters incorporate portions of articles that originally appeared in *American Libraries* in late 2001. Unusually for this book, these chapters include comments from others as well as my own thoughts.

## Library Discussion Lists

E-mail dominates the Internet. Shortly after e-mail began to support one-to-one communication, people began building distribution lists for one-to-several e-mailings. The next step up was list processing, using new software to support many-to-many discussions online. List processors helped people share perspectives for more than a decade and on several networks before the Internet became widespread. Library-related discussion lists also began in the late 1970s. Today, even though we have many other ways to share information over the Internet, hundreds (or thousands) of library-oriented discussion lists continue to serve our need to share and communicate with each other.

You can build your reputation, gain a circle of acquaintances, and hone your writing and argumentation skills through library list participation. You can also mess yourself up badly if you post without thinking or fail to remember that most list postings will be accessible for years to come. You might be inspired to start your own discussion list if you don't find one that suits your interests; that's never been easier to do, even if you're not at an institution with list-processing software.

## Discussion List Basics

Most longtime e-mail users refer to discussion lists by a plural form of "LIST-SERV®," one of the longest-established list management programs—but that inappropriate term is a trademark of L-Soft (which defends against its misuse), and many lists use competing software such as Listproc, Majordomo, or Lyris, or hosted services such as Topica or Yahoo! Groups.

What's the difference between a distribution list you set up for family members or staff in your division and a list such as PACS-L? List processors support larger-scale and multiple institutions and provide some or all of the following:

*Automated, platform-independent subscription and removal.* You can subscribe to (or leave) public lists using any e-mail software on any computer. Many lists require approval from the list owner before names will be added or, conversely, confirmation from the subscriber to reduce spam.

*Managed distribution and response.* Most lists restrict postings to subscribers; some route postings to moderators for approval prior to distribution. When you reply to a list message without modifying the outbound address box, the reply may go to the person who posted the message or to the entire list.

*Special features.* Many lists support a digest mode, in which subscribers can choose to receive cumulated sets of postings rather than individual messages throughout the day. Lists may automatically attach a list identifier to the subject line of each message to help subscribers distinguish between personal e-mail and list postings. With some lists, any subscriber can get a list of all other subscribers.

*Archives and web access.* List-processing software typically archives messages and provides ways to retrieve older messages. Some lists make these archives available on the Web, sometimes with automated arrangement of messages into threads based on subject lines.

How many managed lists exist? More than 250,000 and quite possibly more than half a million, including hundreds within the library community. Let's look at a few.

## Case Studies: Founders and Owners

People begin electronic discussion lists because they see unfulfilled needs. This theme emerges again and again in interviews with list founders, and you'll find relatively few duplicative lists in the library community.

Charles Bailey Jr., the founder of PACS-L, comments: "Mailing lists seemed to me to be a very powerful tool; however, there wasn't a list for public services automation. I felt that there was the need for a list that would encourage discussions on a broad range of topics in this increasingly important area. With the support of Robin Downes (then director of the University of Houston Libraries), I established PACS-L." That was in 1989. Over the decade that followed, PACS-L grew to more than 10,000 subscribers, with more than 18,000 messages distributed and archived.

Nancy Keane, then at the University of Vermont, began AUTOCAT (the largest library cataloging-oriented list) in 1990. The list moved to the University at Buffalo in 1993. Judith Hopkins, co-owner of the list, notes: "The audience is catalogers but that is a broad term that encompasses both those with an M.L.S. degree and those without it who work as copy catalogers as well as in all sorts of roles." If you think of catalogers as quiet, retiring types, think again. AUTOCAT is one of the more active library lists. "It distributes anywhere from 25 to 65 (our daily cap) messages daily. Our messages since 1991 are archived and searchable by subscribers." Tens of thousands of messages are in the archives—more than 75,000 by early 2001.

PUBLIB began in 1992. It's unusual among large library lists in that its two owner/moderators are at different libraries. Co-owner Sara Weissman notes: "The PubLibbers are a great group: over 5,000 librarians from fourteen countries, whose collective intelligence, experience, and humor is delightful. If the rest of the world got along as well as the members of this list, everyone everywhere would be properly clothed, fed, and would live in peace." Co-owner Karen Schneider adds, "this is an incredible amount of fun with very little effort and investment on our part."

Roy Tennant created Web4Lib on UC Berkeley's SUNSITE "because I needed it. I needed it to help me answer my questions about the Web and how to implement it to best serve the needs of my library and its users. From this entirely self-serving beginning, something much greater, much more altruistic was born. This result can be entirely attributed to the participants themselves, who daily demonstrate a willingness to share their knowledge and experience." The audience? "Anyone with responsibility for providing library services or collections via the Web. . . . We are blessed with some very experienced contributors who are not shy at politely responding to 'newbie' questions with useful information. I've learned a great deal, and I know that others have as well."

## List Problems and Pleasures

PUBLIB and PACS-L are moderated, which slows discussions but minimizes irrelevant postings and flame wars. Web4Lib includes more than 3,300 subscribers, each of whom receives a carefully written policy statement upon sign-up. It runs without moderation but manages to avoid either message overload or flame wars.

Flame wars occur when participants in a discussion begin attacking each other. Usenet, one of the earliest networks of discussion groups, has always been known for flame wars. In my experience with PACS-L and a handful of other library lists, flame wars are rare and usually brief. Douglas Winship comments, "AUTOCAT has had only one that could truly be characterized as [a flame war], and that was in the summer of '92. . . . Every once in a while someone says something regrettable, but no flame wars."

Judith Hopkins says of large, active lists: "A supportive library administration is essential in running a list!" Computer centers make changes in e-mail addresses that prevent subscribers from controlling their subscriptions; people forget how to unsubscribe; discussions do get out of hand. On the whole, however, most library lists work remarkably well.

Roy Tennant notes, "What we've discovered from electronic discussions is that one can make one's reputation by the importance and relevance of one's contributions. That reputation can be a bad one or a good one, but once made it is difficult to alter it. If you have a reputation for solid, informative, and thoughtful postings, the readership will willingly overlook a message now and then that should not have been posted. If, on the other hand, you're known as a kook, trying to get anyone to take you seriously will be difficult."

## Posting and Hosting

I've posted to discussion lists for more than a decade, including some posts that turned into articles, some that struck a chord with others, and more than a few that I find mildly embarrassing when I look at the archives. It's easy to shoot off a response to someone without realizing that it's going to the entire list and with the notion that your words are ephemeral. Most of us survive such mishaps.

I recommend library lists both as a way to see what others are thinking and as a way to participate. You should never build a post as long as an article, but it's not unheard of for effective postings to result in invitations to write articles or speak.

You may also find an area where a new discussion list appears to be needed. If your own institution supports new lists, great. Otherwise, services such as Topica will guide you through the process of starting a new list—and, if their economic model works out, will run it for you as well, including the usual range of list-processing options and archiving. If you have a need for discussion that you don't think is being filled, there's never been a better time to address that need.

Before you do, however, check what's out there. One good place to start is Library-Oriented Lists & Electronic Serials, at liblists.wrlc.org/home.htm. It shows more than 300 lists (by topic or alphabetically), offering a brief description of each one and subscription instructions or a link to the list's site. It also includes a brief list of other directories of library-related lists.

Don't assume the new discussion list will succeed. Some lists never become active. Others flourish briefly, then wither. In the first case, your best course is to turn off the list; in the second, there may already be a base of messages worth archiving.

## Library-Related Weblogs

The urge to share interesting and relevant tidbits is natural and healthy. Add jargon such as "collaborative filtering" and it becomes a noble cause. Over the last few years, thousands of people have taken this urge to a new, broader level. With tools to make web page-building easy and encourage the instant updating of pages, these enthusiasts maintain sites that can range anywhere from public diaries to focused citations in narrow fields. These sites are called "weblogs" or "blogs," with the act of maintaining a weblog called "blogging." Some participants see blogging as a movement, some as a new medium, some as a neat new tool.

Weblogs show wild variations in looks, methodology, frequency of posting, and underlying software, but they all have one thing in common. Weblogs always appear in reverse chronological order: today's (or this week's or this hour's) links and comments at the beginning, followed by as many earlier entries as the blogger chooses to show, typically accompanied by date-range archives of earlier segments.

I'm not sure how many library-related weblogs are out there. I do know that I find half a dozen worth checking every day. Weblogs help me keep in touch with outspoken librarians and sometimes lead to articles and sites I'd hate to miss. Some of these sites are a bit casual with spelling and grammar, while others are as professional as any print publication. (Information on some major library-related weblogs is provided in the appendix.)

## A Few Examples

Jessamyn West began librarian.net in April 1999. She notes, "I have always been that person who was talking to people saying 'You have to read this' and this is my way of sharing." She "was working at a small community college library and noticed while surfing that no one owned librarian.net. This was before the blog explosion, so I grabbed the domain name and it was a few months until I found the perfect thing to do with it." West's description shows one effective form of blogging and its benefits: "I use it as a scratch pad for putting links I like about libraries (it started as a place to collect all those 'Sex in the Stacks' and tattooed librarian links). It seemed to fill a niche for some sort of online alt.library.culture scene. It's pretty small—three to four links a day, updated three to four times a week—but it makes it easy for people to browse at work."

LISNews may represent the other extreme of library-related weblogs in terms of form and complexity. Begun by Blake Carver in November 1999, LISNews features full-paragraph descriptions of linked stories with decorative icons, off-the-wall categories, and internal links for expanded commentary and to encourage readers to provide their own comments.

Peter Scott, who has maintained vital lists and directories for library Internet activities for years, began the crisp Library News Daily (more recently Peter Scott's Library Blog) in October 2000 "to keep librarians informed of interesting news items, databases, services, etc.—and to continue testing blogging." Charles W. Bailey Jr., founder of PACS-L, went on to create the Scholarly Electronic Publishing Weblog, the first site I check each day for relevant reading.

Several libraries host their own weblogs, from the Redwood City (Calif.) Public Library to the Waterboro (Mass.) Public Library. Moreover, logs beget logs. Notes Steven M. Cohen: "I first became interested in the 'genre' while writing for LISNews.com (which I continue to do to this day) and looking at librarian.net every day. I wanted to run my own site combining the theories of each one (an informative site with a twist of sarcasm and humor—a salmagundi of library-related information). With the help of my colleagues mentioning my site on theirs, LibraryStuff was launched."

Web audiences define themselves. None of these ventures does formal advertising or targeted marketing (although most of them point to one another when appropriate). Jessamyn West provides a terse and accurate description of the intended audience for most of these logs: "Librarians and library fanatics and information junkies everywhere"—although generally, as Blake Carver adds, "I'd be fooling myself if I thought that was more than librarians."

Audience size can vary enormously and unpredictably. Some well-respected logs have readerships only in the low dozens. Others are visited by hundreds or by more than a thousand unique visitors a day, and some also go out as e-newsletters to hundreds of subscribers.

As with any form of expression, weblogs don't all succeed. I've seen library-related logs run strong for a few months, then cease to show new content. Sometimes there's an explanation; sometimes the blogger just gets bored or moves on.

## Building Your Own?

Weblogs are labors of love, as are so many other volunteer efforts. Several logging programs make it easy. Blogger, one well-known (free) weblog tool, uses as its motto "push-button publishing for the people." A would-be blogger finds web space with FTP access (available free with many Internet service provider accounts), builds a page template (or uses a default), and that's about it. Find an interesting link, prepare a brief write-up, push a button, and the weblog is updated. For a straightforward weblog, you don't need to know HTML; the software takes care of site maintenance.

Should you start your own weblog, in addition to contributing to collaborative logs such as LISNews? I'd suggest looking around to see what's out there and see whether you have something new to contribute. If you don't see what you yourself can offer, to paraphrase the advice of one great radio journalist, "go make some news of your own."

Weblogs offer an easy way to identify and annotate stories and websites that interest you—and to make those links available to anyone interested, without pestering them with repetitive e-mail. It's another way to hone your writing skills through brief annotations and commentary, while building your reputation and serving the field.

# 10

## Doing It Yourself
### *Zines and E-Newsletters*

**K**eeping up with important topics; providing platforms for voices outside the mainstream; offering ongoing perspectives and viewpoints. These needs and motives have always been present; Internet and web distribution lower the barriers to meeting them. Refereed electronic journals may be the most formal examples. Weblogs may be the most personal. Managed discussion lists provide the least predictable and most varied forums.

Free electronic newsletters and zines fall somewhere in the middle, combining the regularity and focus of journals with the personality and distinctive approaches of weblogs. As a preface to, adjunct to, or even a substitute for traditional publishing, free web-based zines and newsletters can be enormously worthwhile. A zine can take you places, put you in touch with people, and involve you in aspects of the field you might never otherwise consider. It can also be a huge amount of work to reach a handful of readers—but look at some of the numbers in the examples discussed here. How many formal journals in librarianship are actually read by as many people as the most successful library zines and newsletters?

## What's a Zine?

Think of a zine as a periodical that's less commercial and more personal and "subjective" than a typical magazine. The underground music scene spawns dozens of zines. Fanzines have been a fixture of science fiction for decades. Today, almost any field with literate writers who aren't readily published in the mainstream magazines will have zines. Electronic distribution and free web hosting by Internet service providers mean that it takes no more than a word processor, an Internet account, and some publicity to start a new zine.

When a publication consists of nothing but selected news items and references to other sources, it's a newsletter. When commentary on those items becomes as significant as the items themselves, the definition becomes fuzzier—and when commentary and analysis break free of the cited items and reflect a distinctive voice, I'd call the result a zine. Sometimes the distinction is impossible to make, and you can just call them free online library periodicals.

Most of this chapter is adapted from an *American Libraries* article written in early 2001. I provide updates in a couple of cases where the situation has changed, include some new personal comments—and add a mention of my own zine, which was not part of the original article.

## Pioneering Electronic Newsletters

Marcia Tuttle, founding editor of the *Newsletter on Serials Pricing Issues* (*NSPI*), notes that it "began as a publication of an ad hoc committee of ALA's (then) Resources and Technical Services Division. This was in February 1989. Its objective, then and now, was to disseminate information on journal prices and methods, and studies librarians were doing to try to have an effect on the steep price increases."

A year later, Roy Tennant (then at the University of California–Berkeley Library) served as program coordinator for Library Technology Watch, "an idea I had to help library staff keep up with technology. The basic idea is that the only way we can hope to keep up with new technologies is to share the work." In August 1990, this effort resulted in *Current Cites:* "Each Tech Watch person was to contribute citations to library and information technology literature related to their program areas." Initially, *Current Cites* appeared as an attachment to UC Berkeley's *CU News* (a weekly staff newsletter). "Soon we created a mailing list for e-mail subscribers. . . . Before long, PACS-L began distributing it on that discussion list."

Both of these early electronic newsletters aimed to help librarians keep up with important topics, and both represented collaborative efforts. Both reached thousands of subscribers and large but unknown communities of pass-along readers. Tuttle notes, "The readership of [*NSPI*] has always been much larger than the subscriber list, which is now at 2,337, because subscribers forward it to their colleagues. Some of the mailing addresses are to library servers and some personal subscribers put it on a local server." Tennant: "We now have about 3,500 subscribers to the *Current Cites* mailing list, but since it is also distributed on PACS-L and PACS-P, as well as available on our website, we do not have a good sense of how large our readership is beyond 'thousands.'"

Every writer and editor would like to reach a larger audience. Roy Tennant looks for "anyone active in librarianship or information technology who wants to keep up-to-date" and believes "our readership could be larger with more active publicity, but when we scrape together the time to keep it going, this tends to have a low priority."

The pioneers keep going because they still matter. Although the formal program that generated *Current Cites* disappeared in the mid-1990s, Tennant comments, "We remain dedicated to the cause that gave birth to it—the necessity of sharing the work at keeping up to date with technology. We simply cannot do it individually, so we must all do a part and share it with others." As to the newsletter's continuity, he notes, "It still amazes me that we have continuously published this resource month after month for almost eleven years."

With little or no institutional support and no revenue sources, most e-newsletters and zines pay their writers and editors in pride and satisfaction. "I am proud," Tuttle notes, "that we were a primary channel of information during the AIP/Gordon and Breach lawsuits. I am especially proud of the e-mails I have received from subscribers over the years . . . and the support of the various editorial board members of the newsletter. I feel like I have 2,337 friends, and that has made my professional life very rich." That recognition can be formal, as Tennant notes: "In 1992, the library of Apple Computer, Inc., awarded the first-ever 'Network Citizen Award' to myself and David Robison, the *Current Cites* editor, for our contribution to the 'circle of gifts' that the Internet was becoming."

*The Newsletter on Serials Pricing Issues* ceased publication in late 2001 after a long and important publishing history. *Current Cites* is still going strong.

# Weeklies

Marylaine Block's marylaine.com site serves up a range of commentary, links, and perspectives, including *Ex Libris* and *Neat New Stuff I Found on the Web This Week*, as well as occasional columns less directly related to libraries. Some of this started while she was a librarian at St. Ambrose University. More has emerged since she quit to become a "librarian without walls," writing and doing Internet training. "I quit my job to become a writer, first and foremost, and mostly what I wanted to do was write about American culture, as I did in both my columns. What surprised me was how much pleasure I ended up taking in writing about librarianship and the Internet."

With 1,100 subscribers (and growing) and 7,000 web page views per day, Marylaine's readership is "librarians of every known type: catalogers, reference, academic, public, corporate, medical, military, legal, and K–12, plus some pure Internet junkies." She'd like to reach more of them, "plus the leadership of ALA and PLA and local and state governments who don't understand the value of libraries and don't fund them well enough."

Rory Litwin started *Library Juice* in January 1998 while he was in library school. "I was the most frequent poster on our school's e-mail discussion list. I forwarded items that came my way from a variety of sources—other lists, mainly. Some of my messages were controversial, because a number of students preferred not to be confronted with political or even philosophical issues, even if they related to librarianship." Litwin "decided to risk seeking a voluntary audience." He got some eighty subscribers right away, announced the service on several discussion lists, and set up a web page. The first issue was "about 40K of plain text, the same as current issues."

Litwin regards *Library Juice* as "an outgrowth of my enthusiasm for the network of people that I became a part of during library school, the ALA Social Responsibilities Round Table community." Who gets *Library Juice*? "A little over 1,500 e-mail subscribers and another couple hundred who read it on the Web. My readers are librarians and library students. They are mostly younger, Internet oriented, and many of them are politically progressive." As an older and more centrist reader, I wouldn't miss an issue. Litwin adds, "I know of a couple of library science professors who use it as required reading in their foundations classes." He'd like to "reach a larger pool of librarians, the average folks who read *Publishers Weekly*." He takes pride in "making it a service that librarians use and know about and appreciate." Weekly newsletters take time, but "it's a joy to do because my enthusiasm for libraries and the library community is constant."

*Library Juice* became a fortnightly in June 2002, with a deliberate change toward more commentary and fewer complete copies of messages that are available elsewhere. The new fortnightly includes links to other items, making it more focused and shorter and improving Litwin's ability to keep producing it while working as a full-time librarian.

# Newcomers and Hybrids

Juanita Benedicto "had been visiting designer websites for a while and admired their sense of community, their passion for the time-consuming sites they maintain simply because they enjoy it, and how they use the Web to collaborate and keep informed on events that matter to them. Then one night, I dreamt of having something similar, told [a colleague] about it, and we started laying down the tracks for *NewBreed Librarian*." Things moved rapidly: "We've had over 10,000 hits to our home page in the first two weeks of operation. We receive e-mail mostly from new librarians and library school students, and then some from librarians who have been in the profession a while."

She's proud of "the quality of the website and the teamwork that keeps it going. It's also given us a professional kick in the pants, inspiring us to keep abreast of what's going on and, consequently, to be proud of the work our profession does as a whole. Most importantly, we've received thank you's from readers who tell us this website provides them with a sense of community that they often feel is missing from their jobs." Carefully designed and providing a mix of interviews, feature articles, and a weblog, *NewBreed Librarian* aimed "to build community, foster collaboration, and create an esprit de corps among NewBreed librarians."

*NewBreed Librarian* was an innovative hybrid during its two-year life (2001–2002). The highly designed site featured a weblog with relatively few entries—but almost every entry was engaging, with clear personal perspectives. The zine appeared every other month as a formal set of articles and interviews on the site.

Then there's *Cites & Insights: Crawford at Large*. As a newsletter, it's not so much a newcomer as a rebuild. As a zine, it's accidental, growing out of a "newsletter within a newsletter" that was also somewhat accidental. I began "Trailing Edge Notes" in March 1995 as the last five pages of *Library Hi Tech News*. It included perspectives too short or informal for my "Trailing Edge" articles in *Library Hi Tech* and a number of other ongoing features that didn't make sense within longer articles: "What you have here is an experiment, one that will probably continue for at least a year." It lasted 59 issues (at 10 per year), for just under six years, half of that time under the name "Crawford's Corner," and eventually grew to 10 pages.

In 2000, dissatisfied with the long lag between completing a "Crawford's Corner" and seeing it in print, I planned an auxiliary web-based "thing" to reach people more rapidly. As I was thinking through that process, the situation at *Library Hi Tech News* changed and I decided to strike out on my own. For a variety of reasons, my original plan for a brief priced monthly (probably reaching a few dozen readers and institutions) turned into a free, longer "at least monthly" that's now reaching more than a thousand readers.

It's remarkably easy to make a web-based zine look professional and "permanent." You can apply for an ISSN on the Web itself at no charge, yielding not only an ISSN but a first-rate Library of Congress catalog record. You don't need to know much HTML to produce decent output—or you can replicate your preferred format using PDF.

I know *Cites & Insights* reaches people because I get several times as much feedback as I've ever gotten for articles in the past—even more feedback than I get for my articles and columns in *American Libraries,* with its enormous readership. Maybe that's because people need to go on the Web and access each issue. It doesn't arrive in the mail at hundreds of libraries, go on the shelf, and eventually wind up in a bound volume with the real possibility that nobody read the articles. I find it likely that nearly 100 percent of at least 1,200 to 1,500 people actually *read* all or part of each issue. When I talk to other editor/publishers of zines, they say the same thing I feel: I can't imagine not doing *Cites & Insights* at this point. It's too much fun and it clearly reaches and informs people—and isn't that what writing is all about?

## Writing Because You Care

People and groups start e-newsletters and zines because they have things to say on an ongoing basis that other people want to read. That may mean collaborative filtering to select the most noteworthy articles in a field and annotate them. It may mean rounding up news in a particular area to provide continuity and focus. It may mean hearing the unheard or providing perspective within a field. Internet distribution, archiving, and other tools can further extend a publication of this sort. *Current Cites* maintains a searchable database to create on-demand custom bibliographies and indexes the full text of all cited articles that are freely available online. *NewBreed Librarian* included a weblog along with feature articles. The *Library Juice* archive builds an ongoing presence on the Web—and *NSPI*'s online archive provides a valuable historical resource.

Starting your own e-newsletter or zine takes a leap of faith, perhaps more so than starting a weblog. You believe there's a field not being adequately covered, or that you can offer significant new perspectives—and you believe you can keep it going on a regular basis for at least a year or two. You know there's little or no money in these online publications; you do them because you care. You care enough to take the initial steps: finding a host, establishing a title, positing a frequency, determining publication and distribution methods, and possibly designing the e-publication and applying for an ISSN. Then you keep caring enough to get each issue out, publicize it, and deal with the fallout.

None of these publications will put *American Libraries* or *Library Journal* or *Information Technology and Libraries* out of business. That's not their purpose. They use new tools to bring new stories to the community, helping to ensure diverse perspectives and informed awareness.

# 11

## Finding Your Niche, Building Your Voice

**S**o you've written two or three articles, conference reports, and book reviews. You're building a reputation as a thoughtful and original list correspondent. Maybe you've started a weblog. Maybe you've spoken once or twice. This may be the time to think about finding your niche and building your voice. By all means do that—but don't discount the virtues of accident.

### Finding a Niche

You started writing because you had something to say. You continue because you enjoy it and you still have things to say. Your first published writing probably concerned a fairly narrow aspect of librarianship. If you continue writing within and around that aspect, you're finding or developing a niche.

Maybe you have things to say in all aspects of librarianship. Why narrow your efforts to one area? Why not write about everything that interests you?

I believe there are good reasons to find a niche for your early writing career. For example:

1. Writing requires reading. Journal articles require *lots* of reading and typically a fair amount of research. When you write within a niche, you can keep up with the related literature and research without spending all your spare time on professional reading.

2. When you publish several worthwhile efforts in a relatively narrow area, you start to become an expert in that area—maybe even a fledgling authority. The more focused your efforts, the better the chance that you'll achieve some recognition for expertise.

69

Once you've established yourself within a niche, you're likely to receive worthwhile invitations: to contribute chapters to books, to write solicited papers, to speak on your topic, possibly to design and conduct paid workshops. It's always pleasant to be asked to do something based on past accomplishments—and invited speeches look particularly good on your vita.

When you're defining your niche, it's important not to be too broad or too narrow. "Technology in libraries" isn't a niche any more than cataloging is a niche; it's a huge portion of the field. "Wireless networking using AirPort" is definitely a niche—but it may be such a narrow niche that you'll find few readers for your third article in the area. Today and for the next few years, metadata crosswalk methodologies (specifically those moving between MARC21 and XML or between MARC21 and the Dublin Core) may be reasonable niches; specific rules for translating personal names between metadata schemes may be too narrow—just as metadata itself is turning into a fairly broad field.

Here's a series of questions that may help you define your niche:

- What can you do (or have you done) in the field that no one else can, or that no one else does as well?
- What do you know or understand better than anyone else, or at least anyone who's chosen to write about it?
- What ideas do you have that are new or unique?
- What perspectives do you have that are different—what do you see that others do not?
- What does the field need that you can offer?
- What have other writers overlooked—what seems to be missed that you can provide?

## A Reality Check

You don't need to define a niche when you start writing, and some of us don't define niches early on. During the eight years after my first article, I wrote about serials keyword indexing; technical standards; USMARC; CRT terminals; RLIN response time; comparative pricing for complete personal computing systems; and PC magazines—as well as a discussion of interest groups in the newly reorganized LITA and a feature review of two books on microcomputers in libraries.

I don't see any niches in that mix. But I also failed to gain much recognition as a presence in the field. When I started taking writing more seriously around 1984, I concentrated on two or three niches. Looking back, I believe early in-depth exploration of a single niche would have served me better, and such focus may serve you well.

## Bigger Niches, New Niches

Don't define a niche too narrowly—and don't stick with a niche so strictly, and for so long, that you're stuck there forever. Even as you're defining a niche, it makes sense to do an occasional piece in a related area or an entirely different area, so you're not pegged as a one-trick writer.

When you feel the need to move beyond your niche, either because it's become passé, you've said all you have to say, or you need new worlds to conquer, you can consider two entirely reasonable approaches—or do both of them.

First, you can expand your niche. Start writing in areas related to your original topic and establish your expertise in those areas. That also works to keep your expertise fresh as a field changes. Some of today's hot topics grow out of yesterday's trends, and you can move smoothly to those topics.

Alternatively, you can start working in an entirely different area. If you've established yourself as a writer, not just as an expert in a narrow field, you'll find it easier to gain acceptance where you've never written before. If I wanted to claim that there was planning behind my early work, I'd call it a deliberate attempt to establish several disparate niches. It wasn't in my case, but it might be in yours.

You'll keep repeating this process throughout your writing and speaking career, unless you let yourself get bogged down in a single area. Expanding to new areas is the best way to maintain your own interest, sustain freshness in your writing, and attract new readers.

*Heresy alert:* I believe that expanding your niches and broadening your interests to wholly new fields is a good idea—but if you want to be known as an authority, it may be a mistake. Think about the people you recognize as The Authority in a particular aspect of librarianship or most other fields. Do you hear or read much from them outside of their own niche?

Maybe depth and breadth aren't wholly compatible. If you want to be known as the world's foremost expert on wireless networking in libraries, perhaps you shouldn't be writing and speaking about copyright issues at the same time. A dysphemistic word for "generalist" is "dilettante."

## Building Your Voice

You began to establish your personal style long before you wrote your first professional article. Your papers in high school and college, years of e-mail, paper letters for some of us old fogies—none of those chunks of prose should have been entirely neutral in voice and style.

You may have been trained to suppress your personal voice by teachers intent on scholarly precision and the standard language of academia. If so, you need to overcome that training. Neutral prose is lifeless prose. If you want readers to appreciate what you write and look forward to more of your writing, you need to write in your own voice.

That's hard to do when you're starting out. It's harder to do in scholarly journal articles, particularly those following the rigid form of hypothesis, literature review, methodology, discussion and argument, conclusion. Even in those cases, however, the discussion and argument section has its own narrative arc and leaves room for style. You may be encouraged or forced to use rigidly formal prose, free of contractions and stripped of first-person and second-person language. That styleless style may be appropriate for journals—but it's probably a poor basis for the rest of your writing.

There should be no conflict between establishing your voice and maintaining good grammar and spelling. I'm not suggesting slang, a return to Dui's spelling principles, swear words interjected into a discussion of serials prices, or argumentation done using the orthography of e. e. cummings. Not that you couldn't get published using such extreme stylistic measures, but going to extremes typically limits your ability to communicate.

I use the word "voice" rather than "style" deliberately. Two people sharing a common approach to narrative arc, sentence length, formality of prose, and actual vocabulary can still have distinctive voices.

There's a lot to be said for studying the voice and style of writers you enjoy reading—as long as you don't adopt their voice accidentally or on purpose. Readers should look forward to reading your articles, not articles written by you but reading as though written by Karen Schneider or Isaac Asimov or Toni Carbo or Roy Tennant, although all are fine writers.

Michael Gorman writes superb essays and delivers magnificent speeches. I recognize his voice and admire it. I would never attempt to imitate it, even if I was capable of doing so. That would deny the strengths in my own voice and cast me as a second-rate Gorman wannabe.

Your voice will emerge most strongly in the rare article that you write in one sitting. You might consider trying to write each section of an article in one pass, to maintain a smooth narrative flow. You should be able to look back at what you've written and spot the sections that don't work well, either because your voice needs development or because they're not what you wanted to say.

As you develop a distinctive voice, you may find yourself arguing with editors. You need to determine which arguments to pursue. Some editors don't appreciate distinctive voices, and they should know their own publications. Some editors lack sensitivity to writing styles, although I've rarely seen that failing in journal and magazine editors. Once you have a positive reputation as a writer, good editors will respect your voice—and will inquire when there's a problem in the style and content of what you've said. Sometimes, sloppy editing or failure to recognize your voice will result in an article losing some of the life and originality in your original. At worst, what's published will read as though someone else had written it. That's life, and I think it happens to all of us—but if your voice is distinctive and effective, it won't happen very often.

## Avoiding Self-Parody

Your voice should evolve as you continue writing. If you're writing out guidelines for how you should write, you may be taking this much too seriously. Voices emerge; only the best fiction writers can set out to design voices without having those voices sound artificial.

Don't let your writing become rigid, following your own set of quirks and approaches so strictly that it reads as a parody of your style. If you want to write self-parody for a specific reason, great—but that's a difficult thing to do, even for writers who are more self-aware than most of us.

Your voice will develop through a combination of accident and design. Look back at what did and didn't work. See where reviewers and editors have had the most trouble or made the most changes in what you wrote. When someone sends you an e-mail or publishes a commentary on something you wrote, and you believe they misunderstood your point, go over your writing from an alien perspective: did they misunderstand because you were unclear?

Don't count on external feedback to hone your style and improve your voice. Many well-received articles generate no feedback at all; many inferior articles aren't worth anyone's time to respond to. When you do get feedback and it doesn't have the air of an ax being ground, pay attention.

# The Accidental Writer

Yes, you should consider a niche when you're starting out—but you should also consider the virtues of accident and be a little wary of setting goals. I won't bore you with the extent to which accidents have shaped my writing and speaking career, but consider the following messages:

> Writing opportunities you hadn't planned for, talents that editors and readers recognize in your work, and areas of interest that grow out of your experience may be more important for your success and pleasure as a writer than the plans and expectations you had at the beginning.

> Goals can be dangerous—not only because you might never achieve them, but because you might.

### *Where Did That Come From?*

In college, I wrote a book-length manuscript on press coverage of the Free Speech Movement. It was never published. While working in UC Berkeley's Doe Library, I worked on a landmark study of the library's success at filling user requests—designing the methodology, preparing the results, doing the statistical analysis. The study was never published (unfortunately; we were doing a much better job than any of us thought).

My first article drew from work experience and my dissatisfaction with a book in a related area. My first published book was born from frustration over the lack of knowledge about MARC in libraries, library schools, and library vendors. The second book grew directly from the first but in an entirely different field (technical standards). And the beginning of my longest series of articles, and the niche that people associated me with in the late 1980s and early 1990s, came from difficulties in comparing computer prices before buying my own. Accidents one and all, at least to some extent.

That pattern continues to some extent. The predecessors to *Cites & Insights* dealt primarily with personal computing topics—but PC issues are disappearing, replaced by broader issues at the intersection of media, technology, law, and libraries.

If I had planned my writing career carefully and followed that plan, little of this would have happened. Instead, I listened to people who suggested article topics and paid attention to my own curiosity in new areas.

The lesson I draw from all this? Plan but accept. Leave plenty of room for incidents and accidents. When people point out something you've done, see whether it shows a talent you didn't recognize. When you're approached in an area you've avoided, or when you become interested in a new area, see whether you should pursue that interest.

Do that and you may forfeit your chance to be the World's Greatest Authority on 802.11g and warchalking—but you'll also maintain freshness in your ideas and writing, and maintain the varied interests and reading that will keep you mentally active as you grow older.

### Milestones and Millstones

Goals can be wonderful—but what happens when you achieve them?

If someone had asked me in 1976 to name my goals as a writer and speaker, I might have said, "Maybe a dozen good articles and three or four speeches." If the same question had come up in 1984, I might have been more ambitious. How about ten books, a hundred articles and columns—although that seems awfully ambitious—and maybe twenty speeches? Worthy goals, each and every one.

Fortunately, nobody asked. More fortunately, I never set goals on my own. Directions, yes: to say things that I felt needed saying as long as people wanted to listen to them; to write things that I felt needed writing as long as people wanted to read them.

What if I had named those ambitious goals? What would I have done in late October 1992 (for speeches), early 1992 (for books), or mid-1996 (for articles)?

Celebrate milestones in your life and career. I haven't done so with any regularity, but it's a great idea. Your first, fifth, tenth book (every book deserves a celebration!); your first, tenth, 25th, 50th article or column; your first, tenth, 25th speech—and your first and fifth keynote.

But don't let milestones be millstones. Recognize that you're doing something right, not that you've achieved a life goal. That goes both ways. What if you set an ambitious but improbable goal—e.g., in my case, twenty-five books, fifty refereed articles, or speaking by invitation in every state? Should I be devastated when I'm seventy years old and haven't met those goals?

# Putting It Together

How would a colleague describe you as a writer? "Jane X writes short, provocative pieces on metadata issues in nonprint media. She always makes me think." "John Y keeps publishing long, turgid reports on new pieces of his ongoing, thorough (some would say obsessive) examination of subject-searching behavior. I wish he'd come to the point some time." "Erskine Z's postings seem outrageous, but they sure do keep the conversation moving forward."

You write on one topic or a set of topics, either building niches or trying to make it as a generalist. You have at least one voice whether you know it or not, and possibly a series of voices for different outlets. Topic and voice: that's who you are, to someone who's never met you. And if your voice is clear enough, they'll meet you with pleasure and relatively little surprise.

Plan, but don't constrict. Don't become so busy with your preconceived career that you can't take advantage of unexpected opportunities—and don't be alarmed when your real talents turn out to be slightly different than you expected.

Dream but avoid explicit goals. If you fail to reach the goals, you may be disappointed even though you've succeeded. If you do reach the goals—what then?

You should know what you think you're good at. But when other people find other talents, pay special attention: in most cases, they see things that you can't see.

Most of all, enjoy and learn—about yourself, about the field, about the ways that fate helps us when we work with it.

# 12

## Overwriting and the Second Draft

**M**ost of us put a manuscript through several rewrites before submitting our first article outside of work. Unless you have a degree in a writing-related subject or a strong background in writing, that's natural and sensible; you want to look good the first time out. You probably rework the manuscript several times, ask friends and colleagues for advice, and rework it once or twice more before you're ready to send it out—and if it's a refereed article, you may wind up reworking it again after you receive comments.

Word processing makes it so easy. You can save drafts under different names (or in different directories, or on removable media) so you can retrieve earlier forms that turned out better than your revisions. A little more polishing can only improve your efforts.

That's great for your first article. What about your third or your tenth? Do you still keep polishing, rewriting, reconsidering, until you're sure you've got it exactly right?

*Heresy alert:* This chapter offers my argument that you should work toward less rewriting. It's an argument that you should probably set aside until you have a publication or two to your credit, and it's one that many library writers and editors will find uncomfortable. To quote the person who reviewed the first draft of this book: "Some might say that professional library literature suffers from not enough rewriting and revision." Some might, and they may be right—but I'm here to argue the opposite.

# Rewriting and the PC

Consider the writing life before typewriters—far enough back that even dinosaurs like me can't remember it. We see the evidence of it from collections of writers' papers, which sometimes include all the handwritten drafts of works.

With expensive paper and the sheer labor of rewriting drafts by hand, it's unlikely that an article or essay would see more than two or three full drafts, although early drafts might have so many scratch-outs and annotations that they're hard to read.

Typewriters sped the process somewhat and encouraged the expectation that a final draft would be clean and free of annotations, but major rewrites were still slow and annoying. While the first full draft of an article might be preceded (then as now) by lots of handwritten notes and typed segments, it's unlikely that most experienced writers prepared more than two or three full versions.

The personal computer changed all that, slowly at first (it was still a pain to do major rewrites with early PCs and slow, noisy, dot matrix and daisy wheel printers), and more completely in the era of the Mac and Windows, powerful and writer-friendly word-processing software, and cheap, fast, quiet printers.

Now—after the introduction of Windows 3.1, Word 3, and letter-quality printers costing $600 or less—you could move chunks of text around, retain more than one version within a single document, experiment to your heart's content, and never deal with the early hassles of producing a clean final draft.

## Overwriting and Life

The sheer ease of revision on a PC has an unfortunate side effect, I believe. Too many writers rewrite too many times, polishing their prose so much that the sheen of neutral correctness replaces the rough spots of the writer's personality and creativity.

Haven't you read articles and columns that obey every grammatical rule, show extensive use of a thesaurus, follow exactly the classic methods for beginning, stating, and ending a narrative—and lie there on the page with no sign of life and no evidence of the writer's personality? I suspect (and can't prove) that such publications result from overwriting: rewriting the life out of a manuscript.

## Aiming for the Second Draft

Here's a goal to consider once you've started to build your path as a writer: submit your second draft.

That's what I do in almost all cases, at least for individual articles and columns. I've been doing it for years, but didn't think about it until the last year or so, when people started asking how I could do so much writing on my own time. My stock (and honest) answer has been, "I'm lazy but I'm efficient." One part of that efficiency is that I normally submit a second draft. Readers don't necessarily see that draft, of course: I love good editing and encourage it. Those who read *Cites & Insights* see something a little rougher, as most *Cites & Insights* material is something like a one-and-a-half draft.

What do I mean by a second draft? Consider these steps:

1. Prepare your material—including your notes, background, whatever. Putting together material and, if you're organized, preparing an outline both come before the first draft.

2. Prepare a clean first draft. For a short piece, the ideal way to do this is in a single writing pass, including the internal revisions and partial rewrites that seem appropriate at the time, ending with a printed draft.

3. A day later, a week later, or whatever suits your schedule, read the clean first draft, marking it up as you read. Be as critical as possible. If you're daring and want external input, circulate that clean first draft. I've had cases where the first draft winds up a maze of red ink and Post-It notes, as I move sections into better order, recognize redundant passages, groan over sloppy language (and sloppier thoughts), and otherwise tear the first draft to shreds.

4. Once you're satisfied with your editing (and saving the original in case you made the wrong choices), prepare a second draft. It might be almost identical to the first; it might be so different that only a sentence or two remains unchanged. You may even recognize that the piece just isn't working, at which point you save good passages as raw material for another round.

5. If the piece wasn't failing when you completed manual markup, you should finish the second round of computer work with a version that reads well on the screen. Check for little fixes, look at length, review spelling and grammar issues—and print it out. Read through the printed version one last time.

6. Send it off and concentrate on your next project.

Note the escape clause in the fourth and fifth steps. Sometimes, you'll find that the second draft just doesn't work. At that point, think of the project as a wholly new article on the same topic, incorporating the good bits from that failure. Do a new outline (if you're an outliner), come up with a new title, write an entirely new introduction. You might avoid looking for "good bits" in the old manuscript until you've done a complete new version. This isn't a third draft; it's the first draft of a new story. That is not a semantic distinction.

### See for Yourself

You have published two or three pieces. You're reasonably confident that you know how to tell a story, how to organize an article—how to write. Why not try the second-draft approach with your next article, or perhaps with an article you've been nervous about writing?

You could try a stupid human trick. Write the article. Prepare a clean second draft. Print it out, stick it in an envelope, and mail it to yourself at work. When it arrives, read it as though someone else had written it. See what you think.

Then compare it to your most recent publications. Don't worry too much if the prose seems a bit less polished; for one thing, no editor has seen the new draft. Look for signs of life, personality, style, voice. Is the new article livelier than your publications? Does it sound more like you, less like a machine? Is it easier to read because the narrative flow is fresh and personal?

Hand it off to colleagues—possibly without your name attached, noting that it's something you'd like them to look at. Think about their reactions. If the ones who know you best come back saying, "Only you could have written this" in a positive sense, you know what to do. Aim for second-draft submission. Save the energy you spend on countless rewrites for new projects, better research, more reading.

You may find you're not ready, that you still need several drafts before you're comfortable with an article. You may never be ready—some writers, including professionals, just don't work well on a two-draft basis. I would guess that quite a few library writers can work effectively with second-draft submissions, and more than a few do so already.

## Drafts and Edits

When I recommend second-draft submissions, I am not recommending that you write an article in one continuous stream, rewrite it once, and let it go at that. For some columns and essays, that process may be ideal. For blogging and list participation, it would be preferable to the rough-draft work that shows up so often. But for many articles and certainly for bigger projects, there's more to it—as suggested by the six steps in my two-step process!

What I call a first draft should be a finished product. Depending on the nature of your project, several steps may precede it. You might prepare a summary weeks or months before you start writing (as I typically do for speeches). You might prepare a detailed outline and revise it until you're happy, something I used to recommend for all writing projects but rarely do any more except for books. You may prepare key paragraphs, citations, notes, background material, mounds of pieces before you start your actual draft.

It's lovely to sit down at the keyboard and pound out 2,000 words of flowing prose. I'm sure there are those who do that. I'm not one of them (although once in a while the muse visits for a 750-word or 1,300-word column), and I doubt that many part-time writers have such easy ways with the language. For me and probably for you, the first draft involves considerable reworking along the way.

"Nope, that sentence just doesn't work there. I need a new subheading here. Darn, I've gone off on a tangent; let's just delete those six paragraphs . . ."

That's all internal editing, and it's a natural part of writing for most of us. PCs make it easy, although they also make it a little too easy to scrap work that might have some promise. Maybe you'll complete the first draft in one sitting. Maybe you'll come back to it over time. Don't go crazy over internal edits; that can kill your prose just as much as doing several full rewrites. At some point, you'll see that you have a clean first draft: rough, but ready to print.

This is the point at which second-draft work comes into play. Set the printout aside for a bit, while you think about something else. Maybe you start on another project. Maybe you sit down for a dinnertime conversation on any topic except the article. Maybe you read a few chapters of a good novel or watch some television. There's a lot to be said for going for a walk, alone or with someone whose company you like—as long as you don't spend the walk obsessing over that draft back on your desk. Get it out of your mind. Let it be, for a few hours, a day, a week.

Now come back to it, reading the draft with a fresh perspective. Maybe you can't pretend it's someone else's work, but you're not the same person you were when you wrote it. See how you like that younger person's draft and what you can do to turn it into a polished but lively final version.

Then prepare the second draft—and submit it.

# 13

## Books

**Y**ou should write books for the same primary reason you write articles: because you have something to say.

A best-selling library book would be considered a marginal seller in the general publishing market. If a trade book sells 5,000 copies in its first two years, the writer is pegged as a "midlist author" at best and dropped at worst. If a library book sells 5,000 copies in its first two years, it's a best-seller. Two thousand copies represent good sales in the library market.

Books in the library field probably won't make you wealthy. They're unlikely to result in motion picture deals. You probably won't have to pay an agent 15 percent, because most library publishers don't deal with agents. But books provide rewards that no other form of writing can.

### A Narrow Field

When you set out to write library-related articles, you have scores of possible outlets, possibly hundreds. With books, that field narrows to a handful. As far as I can tell, the following are the only publishers with anything like a regular program of library-related books as of now, listed alphabetically:

ALA Editions (and some ALA divisions, including LITA, ACRL, ASCLA, and RUSA)

Greenwood Press

Information Today

Libraries Unlimited

McFarland & Company

Neal-Schuman Publishers

Scarecrow Press

The Highsmith Press also publishes an occasional library-related book, as do the MIT Press, ABC-CLIO, JAI, and a few others. The Haworth Press also publishes quite a few books, but they are almost exclusively bound versions of Haworth journal issues. Other library associations also publish occasional books.

Seven publishers and a few ALA divisions: that's your primary market-place. I know that some publishers have mixed reputations, and you can determine those reputations based on your own experience or by asking around. I also know that some publishers get bad reputations they don't deserve. I've talked to authors who say that ALA Editions takes forever to get a book into print—but the books I've done with the ALA were published within a year of contract signing. You hear claims that a publisher has butchered the writer's work during copyediting, but I've heard that said about almost every publication I've written for. One has to suspect that the attitude of the writer has much to do with some of these claims, and that others are wholly justified. I see more evidence of underediting than overediting in library literature.

## Modest Sales, Small Advances

There are few library publishers because it's a small market. There may be more than 100,000 librarians in the United States, but most of them don't buy many professional books—and forty-odd library schools make an awfully small "assured" market for a book.

Modest anticipated sales necessarily mean small advances. Some advances in trade publishing lack any relationship to probable royalties. They are publicity stunts or attempts to retain prominent authors. Neither tactic makes sense for library publishers, all of which are small businesses. Some library publishers don't offer advances at all. Others offer advances in the high hundreds or low thousands of dollars, typically half on contract signing, half on acceptance of final manuscript. These really are advances, not bonuses; you won't see royalties until the advance has been earned back. If you receive a $3,000 advance on a $25 book at decent royalty rates (10 per-cent on early sales, 12 percent at some point), the book must sell 1,200 copies before you see another cent.

You won't get rich writing library books. You could self-publish or try the e-book route, but neither is likely to make your fortune. You can communicate, build a reputation, and have a lasting impact on the field and on your readers. You can make a difference in a way that articles rarely do, because books serve to organize and communicate knowledge in depth and at length.

# Proposals and Process

When I was working on *MARC for Library Use,* I encountered an old friend who'd just published his first (and last) book. He warned me that a book wasn't just a dozen articles strung together; it was much more difficult. He was right (although too many books do appear to be a series of strung-together articles). Fortunately, I had already finished the first draft and was not ready to give it up because of the project's difficulty.

I'm no more qualified to say, "Here's how you write a book" than I am to tell you how articles work. As with articles, there's no single route to a book, although you can read any number of guides that will tell you The Right Way.

## *Defining the Book*

When should you approach a publisher? Before you start working on a book? When you're finished with preparatory work and before you start writing? When you're halfway through? When you have a clean and complete draft?

Yes. Any of those points may be appropriate, depending on circumstances. For that matter, a publisher may approach you with a book idea (particularly if you've established a reputation from your articles or have already published some books), which raises a set of questions I can't even begin to address.

Before you write a book, you need to define the book. One good way to do that is to prepare a proposal, even if you don't show that proposal to publishers right away. If it's your first book and you don't have an expert reputation, you might not go to a publisher at this point; they don't know enough about you and you don't really know whether you can pull it off. Your internal book proposal should answer the following questions:

*What's the book about?* That should require no more than one sentence, and a relatively simple sentence at that. You can add a paragraph or two to flesh out the sentence—but if it takes a paragraph to state the topic, you'll never attract readers.

*What makes it a book?* Why does this topic justify book-length treatment, that is, 40,000 to 150,000 words? If there's only enough content for a booklet, shouldn't it be a long article? Perhaps the best way to show that you have a book-length topic is to prepare your initial outline. If you can define 15 chapter topics each needing 4,000 to 7,000 words, you've demonstrated that your topic deserves book-length treatment. You also have the first outline— but only the first one.

*Why is this book needed?* I could slap together a book on changes in PC and peripheral pricing and quality over the past fifteen years with very little effort. I could put together a book of CD-ROM reviews with no effort at all. But neither book would serve a current need in the library field. (If I'm wrong, I expect a call from a publisher!) How will your book serve the field?

*Why will libraries and librarians buy this book?* A similar question to the one above, but with marketing overtones. For some books, the need is so obvious that—if you can explain it to a publisher—this question is redundant. For others, you need to show the hook: the combination of your reputation, the topic, your approach to that topic, and other factors that mean this book will survive in the marketplace.

*What else is out there?* What's the competition? You need to do a little market research to convince a publisher to take your book, and you should do it before you start to work on the book. You may find that there is no competition or that the last book on this topic was published too long ago to be relevant. A complete lack of competition can be a red flag to the publisher: maybe there's no competition because the book is too narrow or arcane. I stand as proof that a supposedly arcane book can work, and work well: until 1995, *MARC for Library Use* was my biggest-selling and most important book. You may find that someone else just published a book that does what you want to do, and does it well enough that you really can't compete. The most difficult finding is in the middle: yes, there's a recent competitive work—but you'll do it differently or better, enough so that your book's worth publishing. In trade publishing as in commercial television, there's a certain fondness for repeated topics. In library publishing, I believe most parties are sensible enough to recognize the difficulties of redundant books.

*Why are you the right writer—and will you do this alone?* This is a tough pair of questions, requiring more self-awareness than many of us can muster. What in your background, reputation, and skill set qualifies you to write this book—and what in your reputation might disqualify you from writing it? Are you ready to do the whole thing yourself, do you have a coauthor, or do you want to edit a group effort? With the right coauthors, the book may work better. I'm not fond of group efforts—I'd rather get 90 percent of the information in a single voice and coherent narrative arc—but I'm probably in the minority.

*What's the schedule and length, and can you be sure you'll meet that schedule?* Can you do the research, organization, writing, and rewriting for a 75,000-word book in the next eighteen months? Will the book still be relevant when it's ready to publish?

*What about the mechanics?* How will you prepare an index? Professional indexing isn't cheap, and that cost comes out of your advance in most cases. Do you plan to prepare camera-ready copy—and, if so, can you demonstrate that you're qualified to do that? Are you ready to work with two levels of editing, which means paying attention to editorial suggestions but also knowing when to reject them?

Your proposal will include a working title, a one-sentence and one-paragraph gloss, an outline, and answers to the foregoing questions (probably not arranged in Q&A form). Excluding the outline (which may be separate), it should take no more than two printed pages, three at most.

I would treat a book proposal the same way I'd treat a major article. Prepare it, edit it, print it out—and then set it aside. If you haven't done the market research, do it (either the RLG Union Catalog or WorldCat and a major library collection should provide the tools you need). Talk to your colleagues about the idea. Depending on the snicker-to-enthusiasm ratio, you may reevaluate your answers to some of the questions. Don't give in to snickers too easily. If I'd done that, I would have no published books to my credit.

Now pick up the proposal again. Read it through the eyes of a potential reader or publisher. Be brutally honest with yourself. It's discouraging to find a book project failing when you're halfway through, particularly if you've already received an advance. It's much better to spot trouble up front and either solve it or move on to something else.

It still looks good? Edit the proposal, refine the outline, and get to work.

## Submitting Your Proposal

Depending on who you are, whether this began as your idea, and other factors, you might submit the proposal to a publisher before you start actual work. In other cases, you might wait until you're far enough along to be sure you'll do the job—or, less commonly, wait until you're done.

I would be reluctant to submit my first book proposal before I had some chapters ready to show, and I suspect most publishers would be reluctant to accept such a proposal. There are always exceptions, based on your reputation and article-publishing record and on the publisher's needs.

I'd also advise against waiting until you're done. Publishers need to establish production schedules and get out advance publicity; both of those take time. It's likely to be at least a year between contract and finished book, occasionally less and frequently much more. Once you and the publisher are both reasonably certain that you'll complete the manuscript, it makes sense to work together—the publisher preparing the market while you finish your work. (I offer that advice guardedly, since both my first book and this book were complete, at least in first-draft form, before I submitted them as proposals.)

Where do you submit the proposal? It's not difficult to find publishers' addresses. If a publisher has a website, it probably includes instructions for submission. As always, follow instructions. (Information on the author's guidelines available on library publishers' websites is provided in the appendix.)

Submit your proposal to one publisher at a time, starting with the one you believe to be your best choice. Most publishers detest multiple submissions for good reason. You're not going to kick off a bidding war in this low-pay field, and you're wasting the publisher's time if it reviews a proposal and draws up a contract, only to find you've already accepted a different contract.

*Heresy alert:* Some books on mainstream writing provide precisely the opposite advice, and agents frequently submit book proposals to many publishers simultaneously. I don't think that makes sense in the library market.

If a publisher approached you with an idea, you're ethically bound to submit the proposal to that publisher. Failing to do so is unethical and stupid, as it will poison your dealings with reputable publishers. If you've already published one or more books, you'll probably go back to the same publisher unless there's good reason to change. Otherwise, look for the publisher with a book list that seems to suit your title best or the publisher whose books you most respect. Then submit your proposal.

The second worst possibility is that the publisher will turn it down or say you need to have sample chapters before it can make a decision. The worst is that the publisher will keep you hanging for months with no decision or feedback (which happened on my first book). Establish a deadline after which the submission is withdrawn or sent to additional publishers; eight weeks may be reasonable.

## Contract and Completion

The publisher says yes! Here's the contract, ready for you to sign; just send it back and you'll get your advance check.

Not so fast. Read the contract carefully before you proceed. Book contracts are long, and while the publisher may say everything in yours is just standard boilerplate, few book contracts consist entirely of rigid clauses that can't be changed. The following are the clauses I'd look for and negotiate if necessary:

*Copyright.* You do *not* need to sign over copyright and you probably shouldn't. Every good publisher has an alternative clause in which it registers copyright in your name, with certain rights assigned to the publisher while the book stays in print. If they say no such clause exists, consider whether you want to work with them. I would go elsewhere.

*Reversion.* Fair contracts do assign a number of rights to the publisher—but also explicitly cause those rights to revert to the author when the book is defunct. A traditional revision clause might say that rights revert six months after a book goes out of print, if the publisher does not agree to bring it back into print within that six months. But the traditional clause predates print-on-demand, which can keep a book "in print" forever. Print-on-demand publishing is a good thing for both author and publisher, as it can keep a modest-selling book around longer, but it requires care. I'd suggest a clause based on sales—for example, rights revert at the end of any six-month period with fewer than X total sales, or after two royalty periods in which no royalties have been paid, or something similar. This is new territory for all of us.

*Secondary rights.* I can't offer advice other than, "Be aware of what you're signing." You probably do want the publisher to handle secondary rights, which amount to small change for most library books. The publisher's share (typically half of secondary proceeds) barely covers the hassles.

*Right of first refusal.* This isn't always one clause. It may be two or three. One right—the publisher's first call on a new edition of the book and, in some cases, the right to demand a new edition and hire other writers if you can't do it—is probably necessary protection for publishers. The other two rights are not, and won't appear in the best contracts: the right of first refusal for your next book (that is, a separate title) on this or related topics (bad enough), and the right of first refusal for your next book in the field (worse). If you see those clauses, strike them. If the publisher won't agree, find another publisher.

*Schedule and penalties.* When will you submit the manuscript? How long does the publisher have to turn around proposed edits—and how long do you have to make or reject them? What happens if the publisher gets bored with the topic and doesn't bring out the book in a timely fashion? What about indexing and camera-ready preparation? There are no straightforward rules, but you should see to it that the schedule is one you can live with—and that your magnificent manuscript can't wind up sitting at a publisher for years, with no option to take it elsewhere. One special note: If you're preparing camera-ready copy (or the equivalent fully laid-out pages ready for computer-driven platemaking) by agreement with a quality publisher, one that normally typesets books, you should be compensated for that work as a separate fee, not as part of royalties.

## Writing and Publication

The rest is up to you and the publisher. Don't be surprised when you completely redo your outline and change the book title. Expect things to take longer than you planned. Hang in there. If your proposal was honest and your publisher works with you, you'll eventually receive that box with your author's copies. What a wonderful moment!

Then remember that, to some extent, all publicity is good publicity. Bad reviews sell books and good books sometimes get bad reviews. If you did your job well, your book will make a difference. And you'll find yourself doing another book, sooner or later.

Remember this as well: you don't need to write a book to be a successful library author. I can't think of any prominent library author who's never written articles. I can think of several with no notable books to their credit. If your talents don't suit books, don't force the issue.

When it works, it's wonderful. There really is nothing like a print book, paperback or hardbound, to carry your ideas forward for years and increase knowledge within the field.

# 14

## Columns and Series

**A**rticles and books draw citations and build your reputation. Columns add new dimensions: personality, continuity, becoming an anticipated part of a periodical. For the writer, columns demand more attention to deadlines and, typically, more concise writing than articles, but provide an expectation of publication that articles may not. Series fall somewhere between columns and articles.

Good columns represent the predictable core of a periodical—the voices you look forward to hearing from in each issue. Columns are part of the relationship between a magazine or newsletter and its readers (scholarly journals are far less likely to have columns). When you write a column, you become part of a magazine's family: a wonderful role that can also be daunting at times.

## Taking On a Column

When in your writing career should you consider a column? For a quarterly periodical, with a broad topic you care about and length you're comfortable with, I'd say, "Whenever the opportunity arises." For a monthly or a periodical with a narrower topic, you may want a little more seasoning—more experience meeting deadlines and writing to length. While there's no shame in ending a column after two or three years, it hurts you and the periodical when you sign on for a column and miss your deadlines or find yourself repeating topics.

I've seen cases where people began columns with little or no published track record, and others—probably more typical—where the column follows a few years of article publications. My first column came fourteen years after my first article, my first monthly column eighteen years into my writing career. I don't suggest waiting that long. If you have the personality, skill, and ability to meet deadlines, you could start a column at any time.

The elements of a successful column seem pretty clear, no matter what the type of column:

*Timeliness.* Your editor will give you a set of deadlines for the volume year. You must meet those deadlines, which are typically set closer to publication date than article deadlines. When you blow a deadline, you leave a hole in the space planning for the issue and the continuity of your column. The flip side to timeliness is that, for some columns, you can't get too far ahead of yourself—few columns work well if you write a year's worth at once.

*Length.* Most columns have assigned lengths; e.g., 700 to 750 words for single-page columns, 1,200 to 1,500 words for two-page columns. You must be able to meet the length requirements if the publication lays out columns as part of its normal page budget and design. Too long, and your copy editor must make cuts that may damage your prose. Too short, and the column doesn't work. Since columns are almost always shorter than articles, most of us find that columns encourage and require more concise writing than we're used to.

*Scope.* You need to understand the column's topic before you agree to write it and to negotiate the breadth of that topic if it strikes you as too narrow. When I was writing "CD-ROM Corner," I could write a column about distribution problems for CD-ROMs (setting aside the usual review-and-commentary format) but not a column about the advantages of open source software. It would have been out of the column's scope. The original proposed title for my *American Libraries* column was "The E-Files." I said I could live with that but noted that I could already think of some topics that weren't really "e-anything"—for example, "Who Are You to Doubt a Library Legend?" (March 2002), the first column written (although the third submitted for publication). I was lucky: the editors didn't want to limit my scope, instead suggesting the final column name, "The Crawford Files." That would never have happened to me fifteen or probably even five years ago, and it's unlikely to happen with your first column.

*Audience and focus.* Different library periodicals (and ones in related fields) have different audiences. You need to understand the audience well enough to focus your column. My "disContent" column in *EContent* is a deliberate "outsider's view," a consumer and library perspective on the commercial field of digital content. That means providing background material I'd never bother to include in *American Libraries* or *Cites & Insights,* but it also means I can assume the readers' familiarity with a range of digital content issues. David Dorman and Roy Tennant both (I believe) assume a level of familiarity with library operations and needs that they could not assume if their columns appeared in *D-Lib* or *PC Magazine.*

*Personality.* When you read Péter Jácso's columns, you know who you're reading even if you miss the byline. The same goes for Will Manley, Roy Tennant, and Blaise Cronin. When I took over "PC Monitor" from the previous author, it became a different column with the same name. When Joseph Janes continued "Internet Librarian" from Karen Schneider, the focus and style changed. A good column always reflects the writer's personality, even more than good articles and books speak with the writer's voice.

*Continuity.* While this aspect may be a natural result of scope and personality, it's still worth mentioning. Readers come home to columns, in a very real sense, even if they despise (but still read) the columnists. "What nonsense are Alice and Bill spouting this month?" may be my reaction when I reach one particular column, but even that is a form of homecoming. Continuity within columns establishes continuity within a periodical, even as feature articles show variety appropriate to the issue's focus.

*Variety.* Readers expect to read your thoughts within your assigned scope, but they don't want to read the same commentary over and over again with just enough changes so it's not a reprint. Finding variety within your scope may be the most difficult task for a long-term columnist; what do you do when you run out of new ideas? You can legitimately revisit old themes from time to time—such updates can make great columns—but at some point your only sensible option is to call it quits. Before I agreed to do "The Crawford Files," I jotted down a list of possible topics; when that list reached fifty, I knew the column would work.

If this set of concerns terrifies you, stick with articles for the time being. Why not? Columns don't get tracked as frequently by abstracting and indexing services, they're less likely to be cited in other articles and books, and they're not as respectable as refereed articles, at least among proper scholars. A dozen refereed articles will probably do more for your professional career than fifty columns. If columns make you nervous, don't bother.

Why write a column?

> Because columns put you in touch with a community of readers in a way that articles can't, as an ongoing presence in their lives.

> Because columns allow you to comment on themes that are too narrow for full-length articles and also allow you to work individual themes into an overall pattern.

Because columns (at least some of them) let you be yourself much more than most articles.

Because columns can have a cumulative impact that most articles don't achieve, on the field if not in citations.

## Column Varieties

You probably didn't wake up one morning and say, "Gee, I'd like to write a column." You're likely to become a columnist because one or more of three things happens:

1. A columnist stops doing an existing column and the periodical's editor wants to keep the column going. Either your background suits the topic and the editor recruits you, or there's an open call, you respond, and you're chosen. That's how I started doing "PC Monitor" in *Online.*

2. You recognize a need for ongoing coverage of an area, believe you can fill that need, and convince an editor of the need and your suitability. That's how Karen Schneider became the original "Internet Librarian" in *American Libraries.*

3. Your ongoing work with a publication and its editors, taken with your track record elsewhere, leads the editors to approach you about a new column—or ongoing discussion with the editors results in such a column.

There's more than one type of column, even within a single publication. Different varieties of columns require different skills in addition to the set of requirements for all columns.

When you think "columnist," you probably think "essayist," since most traditional newspaper and magazine columns are, in fact, essays. Jon Carroll, the brilliant non-syndicated columnist for the *San Francisco Chronicle,* writes 700-word essays five times a week. Maureen Dowd writes essays. So do George Will, Will Manley, Blaise Cronin, and a host of others. Essay columns are the most personal form.

Given that most of us love to mouth off, you might think that essays are the easiest columns to write. But essays, being the most personal form, also expose you to the world more than other columns—or any form of writing except memoirs and autobiographies—and can be difficult for that reason. When you read "Will's World" or "The Crawford Files," you're not just reading about the topic of the month; you're getting a glimpse of Will Manley or Walt Crawford and how "Big W" (in either case!) responds to that topic.

Columns can also be journalistic, using incidents and quotations to enlighten us on a topic. Few columnists act as pure journalists; most journalistic columnists blend reporting and commentary. Journalistic columns bring a wider variety of voices and opinions into play but show less of the columnist's soul. That can be a good thing, and good journalist columns can serve as mini-articles in a way that essays rarely do. Christine Watkins's "Grassroots Report" is a journalistic column. Karen Schneider mixed journalistic and essay material in "Internet Librarian."

Some columns are reportorial in a different way, consisting largely of summarized updates on a particular topic—for example, David Dorman's "Technically Speaking" typically combines a brief essay with news updates on library automation.

Are standing sets of reviews columns? That depends. Péter Jácsó's review columns certainly deserve the name. My "CD-ROM Corner" pieces attempted to maintain column status by gathering titles into thematic groups and providing introductory notes. In some cases, a standing signed set of reviews is itself thematic but includes no commentary other than the reviews; that's less common.

# Series Notes

Series of articles sometimes happen accidentally, and sometimes they're planned in advance. The key differences between a series of articles and a column include the following:

- Articles are almost always longer than columns, whether they're part of a series or individual articles.

- Readers don't normally expect to see a series appear in every issue of a periodical. That eases the deadline pressure considerably but places the writer at the mercy of the editor, who may omit a series article if space is at a premium.

- Nobody expects a series to continue indefinitely. When I cut off the "Commonsense Personal Computing/Trailing Edge" series after fifty issues, I did so with an explicit ending point—but if the articles had simply disappeared, few readers would have noticed or cared.

Series also have certain aspects in common with columns. Each piece should stand on its own unless it's an explicit part of a two- or three-part set. Each article should be related to an overall theme; otherwise, it's just a bunch of articles by the same author. In some cases, a series of articles carries the same expectation of acceptance that a column does: barring unusual circumstances, you don't expect the editor to reject articles within an established series, and few such articles go through blind review.

It's possible to build a book out of either a column or a series of articles. A book growing out of a series of articles may be traditional in form and content—put fifteen 4,000-word articles with a common theme together in the right order, provide appropriate segues, and you have a book. A book growing out of columns is almost always a collection and reads that way: a bunch of short pieces collected and bound, possibly with notes before or after the original columns. Readers and libraries would buy the series-based book because its topic and content meet their needs. They would typically buy the column collection only because they find the author worth rereading or collecting.

## Saying Goodbye

Every column should come to an end—or at least every columnist's tenure should come to an end. For some natural-born writers, that end comes only with death or disability. Other columnists make a deliberate effort to leave us wanting more, leaving just a short time before they believe they'll start to get stale. That's a tough point to find, and it's natural for a columnist to hang on for a year or five past the freshness date.

With series, it's a little easier. As you start writing more rehashes and seem to have fewer new things to say, good editors will find reasons to feature your articles less often, skipping them whenever there's enough other material. If you're self-aware at all, it won't be long before you recognize that it's time to stop.

Eventually, editors make the decision for columnists unwilling to do so. That decision may grow from reader surveys or from editorial recognition that a column is stinking up the place (or rather, "no longer meeting the needs of our publication and its readership").

When you start a column, it might make sense to suggest a review period—a point at which you and the editors will discuss how it's going, even if it seems to be going just fine. That's in addition to the continuous feedback and annual once-over reviews that should be part of the relationship between columnist and editors. I'm suggesting a known point at which all parties say, "Should we wrap things up?"

Maybe that should happen after a year. Maybe five, maybe ten. In any case, it should happen, although I suspect it's somewhat atypical.

If you're well short of that formal review but you believe it's time to go, give your editors plenty of warning. I'd suggest a year as ideal, but six months or four issues (whichever is longer) seems like a reasonable fallback. If the column needs to continue, that gives the editors time to start looking for a replacement. If you're too tightly linked to the column for it to be taken over, the editor needs to consider the mix of copy and see what should replace your column. In any case, it's polite and good practice to give extended notice before you leave—and to explain why you're leaving.

# 15

# Breaks and Blocks

**W**riters write every day. Would-be writers get that advice from many sources; it's one of the contemporary clichés of books on writing. No matter what, even if you throw it away later, every day you sit at the keyboard and pound out a thousand words. Even though library writing is unlikely to be your full-time job, daily effort is one key to making it work.

## Take a Break!

Writing advisors leave out the next step. Once you've established that you can churn out worthwhile stuff, once you've established a reputation and a following, you need to stop.

Move away from that keyboard.

If you have a weblog, post an "out to lunch: back next week" sign on your site.

Stop writing. Stop posting.

Not permanently—but long enough to make a difference. A week seems about right.

This isn't just a pitch to take a vacation (unless you're a full-time writer). Vacations are different—although I'm also a great believer in leaving your writing at home when you do go on vacation. I'm talking about a deliberate break, a period in which you don't produce.

Give yourself a break and give me—your reader—a break. Let me know there won't be any new content here for a few days.

This advice does not apply to people who haven't yet found a voice or achieved any success. I believe it does apply to novelists and poets as well as nonfiction writers and essayists.

### The Pause That Refreshes

Why take a break? Because you've been working steadily at your writing. Doing that thousand words a day (if it's a hobby); getting new material posted every hour or every day (if it's a weblog). You know you can keep it up—it's become habitual.

For most of us, that leads to a certain loss of freshness. Even newspaper reporters do better work when they see a story with a fresh perspective. Doing the same thing every day encourages bad habits and discourages creativity. Even worse, you may come to assume that readers have the background so ingrained in you by now—or that you're now an expert who must talk down to the ignorant masses who read your writing.

Stepping away from that everyday activity can be literally refreshing. It can help make your prose fresher, the way it was when you were first excited about a topic.

This isn't a theoretical lecture. It's a reflection based on my own experience, both as a reader and as a part-time writer. Typically, I do put in a "thousand words a day," writing, rewriting, or organizing material. Late in November 2001, after producing the final issue of *Cites & Insights* for that year, I began to assemble an index for the volume. To leave time for that process, I got a month ahead of standing deadlines.

I completed the index in mid-December, doing no new writing during that time. I sat back down to write at the end of the month. I enjoyed it more—and I felt able to bring a fresher voice to my work.

# Taking Stock

When you began writing, where did you think you were going? Did you have an express intent other than to succeed? That's an open question for some writers.

Where are you now? Is the direction the one you started with or have you drifted away? Shift happens; there's nothing wrong with changes in attitude and course. But it's hard to notice drift or shift when you're constantly in motion.

Stop, look around, look back at your original plan. With luck, you've grown, gaining broader perspectives and more areas of interest. That's healthy change.

Drift may also mean that the river itself has changed course. When the field you survey changes direction, you need to change approach to remain an effective observer. Sometimes a field transforms itself, and not always through obvious breaks. Consider the typical usage of "convergence" today with its meaning half a decade ago; you'll find something less revolutionary but much more probable. That's partly a matter of deliberate redefinition, but also the reality of shifting fields and trends. The same can be said for "digital library."

You may have drifted in less positive ways. What began as a series of provocations for discussion may have become dogma, assertions of received truth. A corner of your writing may have become the center—even though it remains peripheral to your readers and your intentions. One website that I occasionally visited shifted from a complex web of observations from various thoughtful writers into a site dominated by one prolific and wide-ranging, but also ill-informed and overly didactic, contributor. As a visitor, I lost interest. The site seems to have shifted out from under its creators. If they had shut it down long enough to see what was happening, I believe they could have refreshed the site and arrived at a new center worth visiting. Without that break, the forum became a soapbox with one primary occupant and a declining audience.

## Through the Eyes of Your Readers?

You think you know what you're doing. Stopping to see what you're *actually* doing may help refine that view. There's another, more important perspective: what your readers see.

Maybe your readers want the same-old same-old, unchanging perspectives, fixed attitudes. If so, you need to check your drift and get back in that lockstep. I'd like to think most library people are more open to change. This optimistic view says that readers expect one kind of content but will be pleased to find you've changed in a positive way that's consistent with your original intent but not limited to that plan.

Can you see your writing through the eyes of readers? I'm not sure, but it's worth a try. You're more likely to succeed while taking a break. It allows a bit of perspective.

## Doing It Better

The surest way to avoid writer's block is to keep those hands at the keyboard. A thousand words a day, five to seven days a week, no interruptions, no excuses. That's a great way to start writing—but it's also a great way to make writing a chore rather than a creative act.

Give yourself a break. Look at what you've done and what you're doing. With luck, you'll do it better.

So far, this chapter is a modified version of my "disContent" column in the April 2002 *EContent*—where I recommended that web content sites take breaks as well. I still regard it as good advice for such sites and as good advice for established writers. Oddly enough, it's advice that I take: at least twice a year, I now plan a week—not including real vacations—when I don't do any writing at all. It's not always easy (especially given the peculiar nature of *Cites & Insights*), but I believe it's worthwhile.

# Blocks

You may be lucky. Maybe you'll never sit down at the computer, start to work on an article or a book or a column, and find after two hours that you haven't written anything usable. Maybe you'll never find yourself catching up on household chores just so you don't have to face that blank Word document again.

If that's true and you've been that way for years, let me know your secret. For most of us, newcomers and established writers alike, blocks happen. If you're looking for magic tools guaranteed to break through any block, you've come to the wrong writer; until I started work on this book, I had begun to believe I might never write another book, so severe was that specialized block. I even canceled a contract, something I had never done before.

## Short-Term Measures for Partial Blocks

If you're lucky, your blocks will be like mine. I couldn't get going on a book-length project, but—possibly as a result—I've never been more productive at shorter lengths.

For the short term, there's an easy way to cope with partial blocks. *Let them be.* Move on to projects where you can make progress. If deadlines become problematic, see if you can juggle them; editors are people too. (Don't adopt this as standard practice, but then, blocks shouldn't be standard problems.)

You can try to trick yourself. Work on something else in the same vein as the stuff you're stuck on; set it aside; then see whether you can turn it into a draft for what you need, bypassing your block. Can you expand a draft column into an article, convert a draft article into a column, or turn an existing article into the book chapter that's got you stuck?

Writing instructors have various tricks. There's freewriting—spewing out pages of copy with no particular topic and without ever revising what you're typing. You may find that helpful; I've always found it silly. Some people even suggest copying someone else's work so you get in the habit of typing, hoping that your own words will flow after the guest writing.

## Rejection

Don't let rejection block your writing. If nothing you write is ever rejected, you're probably not taking enough chances. Consider the reasons for each rejection. Maybe the piece just didn't fit the publication; maybe a similar article had already been accepted.

Unless you conclude that the manuscript really isn't very good, you should try again elsewhere (after modifying it suitably). I've been pleasantly surprised to find that a rejected piece for one publication turned out to fit another publication even better after judicious revision.

## Long-Term Measures for Persistent Blocks

What if you're still blocked on something after a few weeks of working around it? Take a break; sit back and think; what's really going on here? In my book block, it was partly the fear of a huge project—but mostly that the book in question no longer made sense to me. Talking that out with my editor clarified the problem.

Reconsider the blocked project. Why can't you get moving on it? Does it still make sense to you? Is it something you agreed to do that you've never been happy about? Does it require a set of skills that you currently don't seem able to muster? What's the problem?

If you can pin down the problem, you may find a solution. With a column topic that just isn't working, the solution is obvious: set what you've written aside under some name like "worthless garbage" and move on to your next topic. Maybe the worthless garbage won't seem so bad in a few months; maybe it wasn't the right topic or the right time. The same goes for articles. If the article was commissioned or solicited, talk to the editor. Can you refocus it so that it works for you? If not, be honest: maybe this one just isn't going to happen—but you'll have something better, later.

It's tough to break a promise. It's tougher to abandon a contract where you've received an advance. Sometimes you have no choice.

# Total Blocks

What do you do when you can't write at all? First, take a deliberate break: don't even think about writing for a few days. Do you have a vacation coming soon? Going somewhere else might help—and leave your computers and notes at home.

Read—not only in your field but also in areas you've never encountered before. If you're a fiction lover, try a genre you've always dismissed or a writer you never had time for. You may refresh your own creativity by learning something entirely new, by seeing other writers at work.

If that doesn't help, it's time to take stock of who and where you are as a writer. Maybe you're so bored with your current specialties that you'd rather stare at the screen than write. If you're that bored, it comes through in your writing. It's time to move to a new area.

Maybe you've done all you want to do, at least for now. Can you get out from under your obligations? If you write articles and don't have any committed speaking engagements, it's easy: just stop. If you have commitments, see what can be done.

Try something entirely different within the field. Is there an interest group or discussion group that intrigues you, but that you've never had time for? Try it out. If you're an academic librarian and can't bear to deal with another committee meeting, think about joining your public library's Friends group.

There's life beyond the library. Take walks. Volunteer for causes you care about (or ones you've never thought about). Take up a new hobby, one you can set aside when your desire to write returns. Get as far away from your writing as you possibly can.

After a few weeks, or a few months, take another look at the writing projects you set aside. Would you like to read the finished result? If so, why not try writing it? Maybe the block has faded over time.

If you look at a writing project and don't have any interest in reading it, what's changed? If you write articles, columns, or books that you don't want to read, I pity you. That's a soulless, cynical exercise that may itself be the cause of your block. But maybe a fresh look shows that your take on the subject isn't what you really had in mind, or times have changed, or it's just faded away. You may be able to reconstruct the project and get started again—but sometimes you'll just have to give it up.

# Calling It Quits

Burnout happens. Some people keep writing (and writing fascinating articles, columns, and books) until they die. Others blaze brightly for a few years, a decade, even longer, and then stop—they're no longer interested in writing or speaking. Some sensible people decide the hassles of non-vacation travel are just too great to justify speaking engagements.

You may find there's no longer a good fit between what you have to say and what library people are interested in reading and hearing. That doesn't mean you should stop. It does mean you should find a new interest—which may mean moving outside the library field.

If you stop writing and speaking because you have more interesting things to do, more power to you. Most of us change directions several times during our lives; maybe library writing and speaking don't fit your next path.

If you're retiring, think carefully about what that means. Abundant evidence suggests that staying mentally active is the best way to stay mentally whole as you age. There's nothing wrong with watching television, there's nothing wrong with sleeping in—but reading, conversation, hard thinking, writing, all these things keep you alert.

Take breaks often enough to stay fresh. Take vacations, real ones, at least once a year—getting away from home if possible, out of the country once in a while. Meet new people, see new sights, eat new foods. Don't call it quits until you've stepped back long enough to be sure it's the right thing to do.

# 16

## Believing Your Own Stuff

**W**riter's block can be debilitating, but short of an actual disability, it's probably the second worst thing that can happen to a writer. The worst, from what I've seen, can happen at any stage in your writing career—sometimes before you even publish or speak.

You can start to believe your own stuff.

I don't mean self-confidence. Of course you need reasonable self-confidence to be a good writer, and maybe unreasonable self-confidence to do keynote speeches. You should believe in what you're doing and why you're doing it.

For that matter, if you're writing scholarly articles or fact-based pieces, you've done enough research to be confident of what you're saying. You have confidence not only in yourself but also in your work. Believing in yourself and the worth of what you write is all to the good.

### The Authority Trap

Problems arise when you become perceived as an authority—and when you encourage that perception and integrate it into your personality and writing.

You will certainly become knowledgeable on any topic you write about regularly, and probably gain recognition for that expertise. You may become known as an expert—and the dictionary lists "authority" as a synonym for "expert." I'd like to suggest a line between the two, but it's a fine line.

> An *expert* in a field has established experience—special skill or knowledge representing (some level of) mastery. A good expert is always

learning from those who are more expert and is continually adding to personal experience.

An *authority* has authoritative knowledge and commands thought and opinion. Authorities provide conclusive statements—backed largely by their personal authority.

If you can't see the difference, that's because I'm neither an authoritative writer nor a particularly expert one. I cringe when I'm called an expert on anything. I reject suggestions that I'm an authority on anything other than the facts of my own life.

## The Self-Citation Syndrome

It's hard to argue with an authority—and that may be the easiest way to differentiate a self-proclaimed authority from a legitimate expert.

A true expert should always be aware of how much knowledge he or she lacks, should look for new perspectives, and should be open to disagreement based on new and different facts.

When an authority is questioned, the first reaction is usually silence: the equivalent of "Go away, kid, you bother me." The next reaction will be to ridicule the questioner and cast doubt on the questioner's credentials. The third stage is typically to reiterate a set of authoritative statements—backing those statements in the best way an authority can. As almost every parent has said, "Because I said so."

One way to spot would-be and self-proclaimed authorities is by the footnotes in their articles: self-citation after self-citation, with perhaps a few second parties added as leavening. It would be interesting to have a citation index methodology that subtracted points for each self-citation, on the grounds that quoting yourself does nothing to strengthen your own argument.

Experienced writers cite themselves from time to time. You don't want to repeat an entire earlier paper when you can reference it and note that it contains additional information and background sources. But I've seen articles and informal documents that are veritable orgies of self-citations, sometimes with no outside sources. After all, why would an authority need anyone else?

## Taking Yourself Too Seriously

You do not know everything there is to be known about any topic you write or speak on. Period.

You are not, therefore, entitled to make wholly authoritative statements on that topic—even if you've published the most important book on the area, regularly deliver the crucial speeches, and have published more articles on the topic than all your colleagues combined.

This is an overstatement, but not when it comes to any area of librarianship that anyone wants to read about. You could conceivably put your hands on every record for some minor historical event and become the world's foremost authority on that event. At which point, the natural response is, "Yes, we've heard all that, get on with it." Even then, new records come along—just as a new generation of Civil War historians is digging through enormous quantities of primary documents that yield new insights into "settled" controversies.

Have you ever heard Clifford Lynch speak or write without an undertone, possibly unstated, of "I could be wrong, but . . . "? If you're in any of the fields Lynch cares about, how can you consider yourself an authority when he is clearly always learning?

Okay, you don't call yourself an authority. You cringe appropriately when the word "guru" is used. But you may still take yourself too seriously—you may still believe your own stuff in ways that will eventually hurt your ability to grow as a writer and communicate with your readers.

It's hard to spot this process, particularly within yourself. Are your speeches becoming a bit pompous? Do you read an article on your topic and feel the desire to respond or become irritated because you could have done it better (and they should have asked you—after all, you're the authority)? Are you treating your readers or listeners the way a traditional professor treats his students?

## Self-Parody

Taking yourself too seriously can lead to another form of self-parody (besides imitating your own style), and you'll probably never spot it coming. If you suffer a serious case of Authority Figure, you won't spot it even when it happens. And you won't see yourself in anything here.

You may still be asked to speak. Lots of people love to hear from The Authority, and after all you probably do know a lot more about the topic than most of them. You'll certainly be asked to contribute certain authoritative book chapters and articles. Will you be contributing to the advancement of the field? Possibly—but that gets tougher as you become more of an authority and learn less about the changing field.

How do you spot self-parody? Ask a good friend. Try to review your work as though it was by someone else—perhaps an unknown trying to make a reputation. See whether you spot the arrogance, unfounded assertions, and general air of superiority that authoritative writing tends to display. See whether it looks a little too much like your style.

## Coming Back to Earth

How do you avoid the authority trap—and how can you escape it if you're already there? As usual, I don't have authoritative answers (sorry about that), but I do have a few suggestions.

*Try something new.* Move outside your supposed area of authority into something where you clearly need to learn more. If you're supposed to be an authority in a live area of the field, by the time you get back to it you'll have plenty to learn there as well. Trying to break into a whole new area can help you take yourself less seriously (there's nothing like a rejection or three to help), and being aware that the field keeps changing will help you move back down from Authority to expert.

*Undermine yourself.* Go back to your first publication in your special area. What did you say that was wrong, shortsighted, or just plain dumb? Where did you miss key nuances? Pretend the writer is someone else entirely (which they are, since you were younger then) and rake them over the coals. Now do the same with one of your recent pieces. Where has intellectual rigor mortis set in? Where did you quote your old self instead of finding new evidence—and did you do it often enough to become a blatant self-promoter?

*Find your weaknesses periodically.* It's not a bad idea to read each new article twice after it appears in print. Once for the pleasure of seeing it in print; if you did a good job, you'll enjoy reading it anew. Then, a month or a year later, reread it to spot the flaws in your work. Critiquing yourself on an ongoing basis is incredibly difficult (and I don't do it that often), but it's one way to keep from taking yourself too seriously.

*Distinguish persuasion from assertion.* It's not your job to tell readers what to think. It's your job to describe the situation, point out relevant facts and sources, offer your own opinions (if it's that kind of publication or speech), and draw your own conclusions. If you're going beyond that to question the integrity or morality of anyone who disagrees with you, you need to back off: you're being authoritative in the worst possible way.

*But I have no weaknesses!* Let's say you go over your first article and can't find a thing you'd change, even after ten years. That makes it likely that rereading your newest piece won't help much either. You are an authority, you know everything important in your area and know how to communicate it, and that's that. In which case, I can only suggest that you roll with it—and don't blame me for failing to take you as seriously as you take yourself.

## Always Learning, Always Human

Two decades ago I wrote a workmanlike book on the USMARC formats. I was lucky; the established experts on MARC were already out there, and I never became a frequent speaker or writer as a "MARC authority." Perhaps I've been lucky throughout my writing and speaking career; I've always worked in areas where there are better-qualified, more knowledgeable people, and I'm always learning from those people.

As a result, I've never been an authority on anything and don't plan to become one. Possibly because of my upbringing and lack of proper education, I don't have an appropriate respect for authority. I was educated at the University of California, Berkeley, not only through frequently superb classes but through the lessons of the 1960s and 1970s. I rarely believe something to be true (particularly something that involves the future or is a matter of opinion) simply because an experienced person tells me it's so.

That cuts both ways. Here I am, telling you that it's dangerous to believe your own stuff, to take yourself too seriously, to consider yourself an authority. Who am I to say that's a bad thing? Maybe it's entirely appropriate for your background, knowledge, and desires to become a "thought leader" and a recognized authority.

If you're convinced that your reasons for doing so are right for you and beneficial for all concerned, then there's an easy answer to the "Who am I" question: nobody you need to worry about. The worst that can happen is that I or someone else will poke fun at you at some point—and you can ignore or dismiss us as the non-authorities that we are.

We will always be human. With luck, we'll always be learning—about any area we're involved in. I believe that process makes you a better writer and speaker; I know it makes you more pleasant to be around.

# 17

# Speaking of Speaking

To speak, perchance to die. Surveys show that people rank public speaking as one of life's most anxiety-causing events—worse than divorce but a little better than death.

I could say this makes no sense at all to me. I've been told I'm a natural speaker (by those who've heard one of my better-organized speeches). What could be so difficult about getting up in front of a bunch of people, some of whom are total strangers and some of whom can help or hurt your career, and spouting off on a topic that you're not really an authority on, knowing that some of those in the audience may know more about the topic than you do?

When you put it that way, I can see why public speaking may cause a little anxiety. An admission may be in order regarding my own natural ease in public speaking.

## "You Must Be a Natural"

It ain't necessarily so—and if it is now, it wasn't always. My first public speech outside work-related affairs was a joint appearance as part of a program, arranged that way partly because I was nervous about being up there alone. That was eleven years after I started working full-time in the library field. The second and third speeches came eight years later, and those combined a colloquium and lecture at a library school, in areas that may not have been fascinating but drew on books I'd already published. I didn't give my first real speech until 1988—twenty years after starting out in the field. I don't suggest you take quite as cautious an approach.

It gets worse. Some time between 1979 and 1988, I did a brief speech related to my work at RLG during a local conference. The details aren't in my vita, possibly because I've suppressed them. My wife was there and can attest that I was nervous and came off that way.

Eventually, I started speaking on a broader range of topics and with a little more ease—which doesn't negate the nervousness or terror I felt before each appearance. Some first-rate public speakers become physically ill before each appearance. Others use beta blockers or other drugs to help them get on stage. I've never gone that far, but I'm not in that category of speaker.

Final admission, since this isn't a confessional: I had less excuse than you do for being nervous about speaking and for putting it off so long. I was active in the National Forensics League throughout high school, spending many weekends in speech tournaments somewhere in California's Central Valley, doing combinations of debate, extemporaneous, and impromptu speeches. I'd been speaking in front of strangers for four formative years.

It's not the same. Speech tournaments have judges but few spectators—and neither the judges nor the spectators have much to do with your career plans.

## Speaking Out

Don't wait twenty years—and don't wait until you're sure you'll be calm. The first is cowardly, the second improbable. But consider: you must have done verbal presentations during college and graduate school. You didn't die. You probably won't out in the field, either.

Speeches do cause more anxiety than writing. Why shouldn't they? When you publish, you're communicating one-on-one with the reader. You can correct mistakes. Uh, you're unlikely to, uh, pepper a written manuscript with, um, like, awkward pauses. If you're stalled, you can set the article aside until later. You can assume that your first few topics are so narrow that only the editor and a dozen specialists will ever read them—and in most cases, you won't get enough feedback to be sure that's not true. At the same time, your readers set their own pace in dealing with your material. If your writing is concentrated (saying a lot in a few words), readers who find the topic worthwhile can go back to get more out of it. If your writing is soporific, you don't actually see people nodding off. You can expand on points in textual footnotes and back up your arguments with citations.

When you speak, your audience is right there in front of you. It's tough to make editorial corrections while you're speaking and impossible to undo your errors completely. If you toss out too many ideas in a short span or assume too much prior knowledge, you lose part of the audience. If you spread things out too much or spend too much time on the basics, you lose the rest of the audience (and may inadvertently insult some of them). For an early afternoon speech, it's hard to know whether those declined heads mean rapt concentration, the aftereffect of heavy lunches, or the possibility that you're not reaching the audience. What you say is what they get, although you can always use handouts for added material.

Persevere. It makes sense to start speaking for audiences outside work around the same time you start writing for publication. Just as you route early manuscripts to friends and colleagues for comments, there's nothing wrong with testing your speeches on a voluntary audience of coworkers: I know people who still do that after thirty years in the field.

# Why Speak?

Public speaking causes anxiety. Things can go wrong. What's more, it's an inefficient way to reach people. In a state library conference, you may be speaking to fifty people or fewer; even at an ALA conference, it's unlikely you'll reach more than a few hundred. The largest group I've ever addressed was 600 Australian librarians; at the other extreme, I've spoken to groups of a dozen.

Even my own little zine reaches twice as many people as the best-attended speech I've ever made. Most journals and magazines I publish in reach ten times as many as that, or more—right up to *American Libraries* with more than 63,000 readers. In other words, each article and column in *American Libraries* reaches more people than all the speeches I've ever given.

So what's the point of speaking?

Speaking reaches people in different ways than writing, even for those who learn equally well from both methods.

When you speak, you can't help but have your own voice. Even the most structured presentation shows some of your personality. People get to know who you are in ways that writing can obscure.

Speaking encourages interaction—questions and answers, discussions in the hallway, debates in the nearest bar or lounge. You can expand on points, learn where people misunderstand what you have to say, hear different perspectives.

Finally, when you begin to speak outside your primary associations, speaking puts you in touch with people you might otherwise never meet and can open aspects of librarianship and practice you wouldn't otherwise see. I love to speak at state and regional library conferences because I get to meet practicing librarians beyond the specialists I see at the ALA Annual and Midwinter conferences, and because I can attend programs and learn more about real library problems than I would at the national level.

# The Classic Structure

If traditional scholarly journal articles follow a fairly rigid structure, so do traditional topical public speeches. You probably know the drill:

> Tell the audience what you're going to tell them (the introduction). Tell them what you have to say (the body). Then tell them what you just told them (the closing summary).
>
> Have a single topic with no more than three subtopics.
>
> Begin with a joke or two to loosen up the audience. Nothing eases tension better than a good laugh. End with something stirring for them to remember.
>
> If you can't say it in twenty or thirty minutes, it's probably too complex for a speech.

Do these rules make sense? Yes and no—and when I say "no" it's from the perspective of a frequently untraditional speaker who doesn't always delight his audiences. If you want intensive coaching and experience in traditional speaking, go join Toastmasters—a sincere suggestion that's a little too late for me. Those groups can help you see how to carry out the traditional approach so that it's lively and communicates well.

The traditional structure exists for a reason: it works. Elements of that approach work for most speeches. The entire approach works for many topical speeches.

Saying that, I must also say that I've always disliked "starting with a joke" and I never do. This is partly because I'm not skilled at delivery; mostly it's because I find the approach artificial. Anecdotes need not be jokes. If an anecdote is true to life and speaks to the topic or to the circumstances of your appearance, it can be a good way to start.

Laughter is a good thing when it's with you. It's debilitating when you become aware that they're laughing at you. I don't do jokes, but I have always seen the virtue of pointing out the humor inherent in so many areas of librarianship. Half an hour of unrelieved irony is shtick, suitable for stand-up comedy but not for professional programs—but an occasional ironic touch can leaven a serious talk without weakening it.

The three-times approach to organizing a speech makes excellent sense for most topical speeches. The adage "What I tell you three times is true" is both folklore and reality. By presenting your key points up front, amplifying them in an organized manner, and repeating them in a differently worded summary, you drive home those points.

Limiting a topical speech to one primary topic with a handful of subtopics also makes excellent sense, particularly when combined with the ideal 15- to 30-minute length for most topical speeches. An audience can only absorb so much at once, particularly since most topical speeches appear clustered within related programs.

You should learn the rules for public speaking. That way, if and when you break them, it won't be entirely accidental.

## Categories of Public Speaking

The range of possible speeches is nearly as broad as the range of publishing possibilities. I see three axes by which to categorize typical library public speaking: arrangements, formality and structure, and length and approach.

### Arrangements

There are two primary categories here: arranged and invited speeches. You'll probably begin with arranged speeches (unless you postpone speaking until you're already an authority), and you'll probably take special delight in invited speeches.

Arranged speeches include those where you've helped plan a program; cases where you've applied to present a paper at a conference; and cases where you're speaking because your organization was asked to send a representative.

Invited speeches include keynotes and plenary single-speaker programs, but also participation within programs and programmatic conferences, and paid workshops for those who do such workshops well.

With relatively few exceptions, arranged speeches are done at your or your organization's expense. You can make your case and build your reputation, but it's rare that you'll be covered for expenses, much less offered an honorarium. (There are always exceptions.)

When someone invites you to speak, it's reasonable to discuss expenses, honorarium, and other issues. I've never had a set fee and have always been uneasy when a potential invitation comes with a "name your fee" request, but I understood early on that invited speeches should include expenses and an honorarium. You may never know whether you're charging enough. You'll know if you're charging too much because invitations will fall through.

## Formality and Structure

While it's reasonable to assume that you'll begin with arranged speeches that are part of programs and may move on to single-speaker programs and keynotes later in your career, variations in formality and structure will continue throughout your career, with no particular logic. For example:

1. The least formal and unstructured public appearances include leading a discussion and participating in an informal panel, where there's a topic but no set speeches.

2. One step up in formality and a big step up in anxiety come in responding to a speaker as part of a response panel, particularly when you're not provided with an advance text.

3. Most library speeches fall into a middle ground. You may be one speaker in a topical program with a prearranged specific topic and time slot, perhaps following a set of individual speeches with an open discussion period. You may be presenting a paper as part of a group of related (or unrelated) papers, where your speech itself will be more structured but will have little or no relationship to the other speeches.

4. Next comes the flip side of responding to a primary speaker—being the primary speaker with a group of respondents. At this point, you must have an established reputation, and I've never been sure whether it's more distressing to be responded to or to be a respondent.

5. Then there's the keynote or single-speaker session. It's just you and the audience. Very few people have heart attacks while delivering keynotes, although some of us feel as though we'd like to.

6. Finally, there are formal workshops, training sessions, and oddities such as teleconferences. Your role in these events is likely to be even more structured than speaking as part of a topical program, but you're also likely to have better support mechanisms. You can make serious money presenting workshops—or so I hear.

## Length and Approach

Explain USMARC-XML metadata crosswalks. You have five minutes.

That's an extreme—like being asked to do a full-day workshop on "tradition and technology in tomorrow's library" twice over two days in two different cities, when you've never done a workshop or been in the state. The first scenario is unworkable for most mere mortals. The second is interesting, but not entirely implausible: I've done it once, but probably won't do it again.

Otherwise, it's unusual for a speech to run less than 10 minutes or more than 75 minutes. Most papers or speeches within topical programs run 15 to 30 minutes, while keynote and other single-program speeches may run 40 to 75 minutes. Sessions within a multiday workshop may be 75 minutes or longer, but that almost always includes time for discussion. Responses to a speech may be 10 minutes or shorter, while statements within a panel or segments of a debate format might be as short as 5 minutes each.

Realistically, you should expect most keynotes and plenary speeches to run roughly 45 minutes, most topical presentations to run roughly 20 minutes. Chances are, you'll speak at 80 to 125 words per minute. Any faster than that, and you're rushing. So a 20-minute speech is equivalent to a 2,000- to 2,500-word paper (or, roughly, one of these eight-page chapters); a keynote may include 5,000 or 6,000 words.

# 18

# Hiding behind PowerPoint

When I first outlined this book, I had five chapters on speaking. The second outline had three chapters—and in the writing, one of those disappeared. It's hardly surprising that, as Danelle Hall notes in "A View from the Back Wall," a three-year search of Library Literature "turned up only a handful of articles on the subject of public speaking."[1] Why?

Many comments I could make about public speaking have already been made about library writing, since the most common forms of library-related speaking you're likely to do—contributed papers and topical speeches—are analogous to articles both in length and form.

Hall's article provides a well-stated set of rules for presentations. I'll note some of those rules later, but also note when I believe you can break the rules.

First, a few notes on discussions, keynotes, and originality vs. repetition—the remnants of that third chapter.

## Discussions

Leading a focused discussion may have nothing to do with public speaking—or, in some cases, you might be asked to kick off a discussion with a brief commentary on the issues. In either case, your primary goals should be five-fold:

1. Introduce the topic and, as needed, gently guide the discussion back on topic when it strays.

2. Encourage participants to take part without resorting to artificial methods such as explicitly asking someone to speak up because they've stayed silent.
3. Discourage one or two participants from dominating the discussion— particularly difficult when you have big-mouth, self-important people in the discussion—without alienating the know-it-alls or destroying the flow of conversation.
4. Listen more than you talk. When you begin a discussion, and particularly when you're listed as a key participant, it's all too easy to be the dominant voice, turning an open discussion into a question-and-answer session.
5. Avoid personal attacks and incendiary remarks, both your own and those of others.

These aren't always simple goals to achieve. Experienced discussion-session people may note a sixth goal for many such sessions, one that I deliberately omitted:

6. Take good notes so that you can prepare a summary of the discussion for distribution among the group, posting on appropriate websites, or inclusion in a newsletter.

I don't believe that a discussion leader should also attempt to take notes. Instead, someone else should agree to serve as note-taker, unless someone's willing to record the session and attempt to produce notes from the recording. That's a chancy process at best.

## Keynotes and Plenary Speeches

You can have a long, worthwhile career as a library public speaker without ever doing a keynote. What you usually *can't* do is give a keynote because you've always wanted to. Keynotes are almost always invited speeches, although I suppose you could organize your own conference if you're sufficiently intent on doing a keynote.

Keynotes and plenary speeches differ from typical speeches in several ways, in addition to the implausibility of proposing that you do a keynote:

Keynotes and plenaries tend to be longer than other speeches, running 40 to 60 minutes (sometimes longer) instead of the typical 20 to 30 minutes.

Keynotes are almost always more personal in tone than topical speeches and contributed papers. You're speaking to people, not simply delivering a speech, and they asked *you* to speak, not "some person who knows something about topic x."

Keynotes can cover more ground than typical speeches, although some of us may overdo it. I'm probably one of the worst offenders in the field, with keynotes that sometimes include four or five major themes, but I've heard better keynote speakers cover two or three distinct themes in a single magnificent hour.

Good keynotes can and should dispense with PowerPoint and other audiovisual aids in most cases. A keynote should be you and the audience, with technology assisting only to make you audible and visible to everyone there.

## Originality and Repetition

Should you prepare each new speech from scratch, or should you give the same speech repeatedly? As with so many choices, the best answer is "Yes."

Yes, you can and should repeat the same speech when you have a carefully prepared presentation that people want to hear in many different cities on many different occasions. There is a limit, though, one that I've heard exceeded more than once. Canned speeches eventually go stale, because the world changes and because you tire of delivering the same speech. In both cases, the audience will recognize the problem—but you should spot it first and either take a break from the topic or update the speech.

Yes, you should prepare each new speech from scratch when you're being asked to do a keynote or something specific to a particular conference. I don't really mean that, of course. If you speak more than once or twice a year on similar topics, you're unlikely to write an entirely original speech on each occasion. Realistically, you should ensure that each new keynote and plenary speech is distinctive and has some new material. I try to ensure that each new keynote is at least 30 percent new material or material I haven't used in two or three years, although the circumstances of the speech can increase that percentage.

There's nothing wrong with using your published articles in your speeches. Some of the people who invite you may explicitly ask you to do so. It is a little tawdry, I believe, to simply read a previously published article and call it a speech, unless the inviting parties know that's what you plan to do. I attended one conference where a very well-paid keynote speaker began by presenting a ten-minute commentary that the person next to me recognized (word for word) from its published form. The speaker then said, "Let's hear your ideas," and that was it for an hour-long slot. Several thousand dollars plus expenses for absolutely no effort: where can I get gigs like that? If you have the ethics and creativity of most librarians, you wouldn't do that if you could, and I certainly don't suggest it.

The Web makes the situation a little more complicated. When you speak at a conference, you may be asked to provide your notes (or your PowerPoint slides or your full-text draft) for the conference website. It may even be a requirement. I've agreed when asked, always with the caveat that the written draft of my keynote-style speeches doesn't necessarily have much in common with what I say.

The tricky part here is that once it's on the Web, your carefully prepared speech is out there. People going to the next conference you speak at may Google you (or Teoma you, if you prefer) and come upon the web version. When you deliver the same speech they've just finished reading, they're likely to be a little disappointed.

I'm not sure there's much you can do about that. You can be honest, and that helps—for example, your handout might note that the speech was originally prepared for another conference. Partial overlap is another issue. Some listener disappointment can't be avoided.

## The PowerPoint Problem

The first time I spoke outside the United States was as the first of five keynote speakers (two each day, with the group as a closing panel) for a major Australian library conference. We all received the instructions for speakers, which included two mandatory elements:

1. We were expected to provide a written text in advance (formatted to specific guidelines) to appear as part of the conference proceedings that each attendee would receive at registration.
2. All presenters were expected to use PowerPoint. Each speaking venue was guaranteed to have both a Windows and a Macintosh computer hooked up to a professional-grade data projector.

I managed to acquire A4 paper (a slightly different size than American letter paper) to satisfy the first requirement. No problem. Then I sent a message to the conference managers regarding the second requirement. "I don't use PowerPoint, particularly for a keynote." They responded that the requirement could, of course, be waived for keynotes. I wasn't the only prima donna. Two other keynote speakers wanted to speak directly to the audience without the aid of presentation software.

I still don't use PowerPoint or other visual aids in speeches, keynote or otherwise, unless it's clearly necessary (for example, if I'm talking about web pages or typefaces, I have visuals of them). That's probably a mistake for non-keynote speeches, and it's not a practice I suggest you follow. Most of the time, for most regular speeches, your audience will expect PowerPoint or an equivalent and you'll want to use it.

I have two problems with PowerPoint and equivalents, one personal and one that I regard as legitimate. The second appears as the title for this chapter.

The first is a combination of laziness, disorganization, and flexibility. I'm too lazy to carry a notebook computer to conferences and don't own such a device. I could bring along a diskette or CD-R with PowerPoint slides, but I wouldn't be able to change them on the spot. Disorganization and flexibility are two sides of the same coin. More than half the time, I substantially rebuild my speech both on the morning of the speech and during the speech itself. The first is tough when you're using PowerPoint, and I've seen hilarious results when people do revisions half an hour before a speech. The second is nearly impossible. You wind up disrupting the flow of the speech while you attend to the mechanics of finding the right slides.

The second problem with PowerPoint applies to any visual assistance that you use throughout the speech. Too many speakers hide behind PowerPoint, "speaking to the screen" to minimize the nervousness of speaking to an audience. Too many others spell out the entire speech in an endless series of slides, reading the PowerPoint slides and providing little to interest the audience.

I understand the temptation to "speak to the screen" and the soothing knowledge that with the lights down, you don't know who's falling asleep or has decided to walk out. But in avoiding nerves you've also avoided contact. Sitting in a dark room staring at a set of bullets on the screen, I wonder why I'm not just reading an article or—better yet—watching television.

This disconnect is not a necessary consequence of using PowerPoint. Quite a few speakers use PowerPoint to anchor their speeches but maintain an audience connection, communicating brilliantly. I have seen more good speakers using PowerPoint than speakers evading their audiences, but I've also seen good speakers who I thought would have been more effective if the projector was off and the lights were up.

## Doing It Right

If you're going to use PowerPoint, do it right, as summarized in Danelle Hall's article. Start with a title slide (your name, title, and affiliation and the title of the speech); keep the slides simple, with big type in high-contrast color combinations; don't overload any slide; and have a backup strategy in case the technology crashes.

You can use transparencies instead of PowerPoint, and you may want them as backup, but you must pay attention to type size (probably 30-point minimum on a regular transparency) and simplicity (lots of space, few lines, few words per line) as well as clarity (a simple serif or sans serif typeface, always upper and lowercase). Twelve-point type (typewriter-size) on a transparency is the kiss of death, although it's just fine for handouts. Better you should turn off the overhead projector and just talk.

If you're part of a multispeaker program, work with the moderator or the other speakers so that all of your PowerPoint presentations are on a single computer—maybe even as sections of a single file. While it can be amusing to watch the intermittent chaos as each speaker in a program tries to find the right notebook computer among the four littering the podium and figure out how to move the projector connection to that notebook, it disrupts the flow of the program and takes time that could be better used for speaking or questions.

Hall also provides useful comments on checking out your speaking location, ones every speaker should heed. Read the article: it's short, very well written, and followed by an equally short and well-written Janet Swan Hill piece on what hosts should do to make guest speakers happy.

Visit the room in advance, checking out the lighting, podium, and other arrangements. You can't always do this more than ten or fifteen minutes before your speech, as conference room arrangements may change several times a day, but you don't want to be surprised by the set-up.

Did I mention timing your speech? Do a complete run-through at least once, including PowerPoint. If you use a preview audience, make sure that you're speaking at a reasonable pace (ask them!) and that you've left a little slack time. If you don't use a preview audience, add at least 20 percent to the time you think you're taking.

## Coping with Surprises

Expect surprises and know how to handle them. If you're the fourth 15-minute speaker in a 75-minute slot (with 15 minutes reserved for questions), don't be surprised when you're left with five minutes of time. You're allowed to curse the self-important blockheads ahead of you who took 20 or 25 minutes each, but only under your breath. Know where you can cut at the last minute—and if the situation's completely hopeless, say so up front.

What will you do when there's no podium to rest your detailed notes on? In one case I still remember with horror, I should have refused to give the speech, but that's rarely an option. If you're there early, you can make your needs known—and point out that these are needs you communicated quite clearly to your host both when you agreed to speak and in a follow-up message shortly before the conference.

How do you present a fully written speech so that it doesn't look or sound like you're reading it? Memorization is good if you're up to it; otherwise, you need a combination of large type with loads of spacing, style, and luck.

What do you do when none of the technology works and your handouts didn't arrive? You deliver a brilliant speech that leads to happy listeners and lively discussion. In my experience as a listener, quite a few speakers surprise themselves when they're forced to do without props—almost always for the better. I've seen very few meltdowns in such cases, except when the speaker is so intent on restoring the technology that the aim of the speech is forgotten.

You're speaking because you have something to say. If you care about what you're saying, you'll survive the surprises—and probably do a better speech as a result.

NOTE

1. Danelle Hall, "A View from the Back Wall," *American Libraries* 33 (May 2002): 64–65.

# 19

# Who Are You— and What's Next?

**W**hat happens when you succeed as a writer and speaker? You'll probably win an award or two. If you're primarily a writer, you'll be asked to speak. If you're primarily a speaker, you may be asked to write.

Your writing and speaking may improve your situation at your day job— or may not be recognized where you work. If you stick with it, you can earn enough from spare-time writing and speaking to make a difference: an extra cruise every year or two, a new car once or twice a decade, better food and wine on the table, better clothes on your family's back.

You may even wind up in *Who's Who in America* on the basis of your writing and speaking. I'm absolutely certain that can happen, although it's always difficult to tell why you're chosen for that particular honor.

And you may find the questions that head this chapter totally absurd. You know who you are, and your writing is an extension of yourself. What's next? You'll keep on doing it, gaining more honors and glory and communicating to more people.

Congratulations. Don't let me suggest otherwise. If you have the confidence, drive, and assurance that you're understood the way you want to be understood, you're probably a better writer than I am anyway.

For some of us, however, who we are—our public persona—isn't necessarily who we set out to be. That's what this chapter is about.

## You Are What People Think You Are?

If your writing and speaking have any personality at all, you'll eventually get direct or indirect feedback suggesting what people think you are. This is particularly true when you write a book, as reviewers tend to include an offhand summary of the writer in discussing the book itself. "Janet Serendipity, recognized authority on nonprint cataloging and e-book appliances, takes us by surprise with this masterpiece on research techniques for measuring online catalog usability."

These snap summaries can also happen in publicity for speeches, in introductions for speeches, in other articles and books that cite your articles and books, and in discussion list postings and weblogs. "As noted champion of free speech Joseph Explorer said in a recent article . . . " "I must take issue with Ralph Terrace despite his standing as a renowned expert on library signage." Or, for that matter, "Once again, Walt Crawford is whining about new technology and pining for the good old days." (All quotes imaginary—including, I believe, the last one.)

Pay attention to these offhand comments, whether they refer to your areas of expertise, your attitude, your style, or your depth of knowledge. If you maintain a clipping file, remember that rants may be more important than raves. Even if you don't keep clippings (which, for "e-clippings," can be a nuisance) or maintain them selectively, think carefully about the shorthand being used to describe you.

With rare exceptions (usually ad hominem cases where the reader or listener has an ax to grind or is a known crank), every snap summary is true—or at least part of the truth. You need to triangulate a given remark with other remarks made by the same person about other people you know, but that only refines what's been said.

Maybe all the comments strengthen the sense you already have of who you are and what you're doing. That's less helpful than comments that take you by surprise—and might make you wonder whether you've defined yourself too narrowly. Are you still capable of surprising your readers and listeners? Do you want to be that predictable?

What do you do with surprises? That depends on the surprise, of course, but also on your own desires. For example:

1. When you're labeled as an expert in an area you've barely thought about, consider whether it's an area you should pursue more avidly. Apparently you're touching a nerve. If the comments are both surprising and favorable, you might think of doing more articles, more speeches, or even a book in that area. Achieving recognition when you've just begun is an unusual gift, easy to squander but wonderful to use.

2. When you're noted for work that you consider wholly outside your interests, try to find out why. It could be simple confusion—someone with a

similar name, someone else who spoke on the same program as you, someone in the same organization. Or is something else going on? Did you comment on an area incidentally, in the course of some other work? If so, is it an area you want to pursue? (I've sent people e-mail in cases like this, admitting that I've forgotten where or when I wrote or spoke on a topic. The responses have been enlightening—and have resulted in some later articles. And yes, in a couple of cases, it was pure confusion. For example, I'm not Gregory Crawford.)

3. What if you're being labeled as a wannabe, phony, or inadequate in an area you believe you understand thoroughly? You need to know more about the person making the charges. Then you need to look back at your work and consider the possibility that he or she is right.

4. Some readers can't cope with discussions that offer more than one side of a story. Say that library portals have considerable advantages but also have limitations, and you may be attacked for tearing down library portals. Say that e-book appliances don't seem likely to replace print books and that e-books seem likely to succeed in specialized markets rather than as wholesale replacements for print books, and you may be accused of saying that there's no place for e-books. In these cases—which are, unfortunately, numerous—you should consider whether you're writing clearly enough, but also consider that some people can't deal with ambiguity. You can choose to become doctrinaire, always stating cases in black and white terms, or you can accept that you'll be misunderstood by some readers.

## You Are What You Choose to Be

You can take advantage of surprising feedback, and you should pay attention to negative feedback. But while many of us don't have the luxury of being precisely who we set out to be, you don't need to be what people think you are.

If you're unhappy with your apparent writing and speaking persona, change it. Determine why you're being misunderstood. Correct the problems, when they are problems. If you're being called a guru in an area that no longer interests you (or never did), leave it alone and increase your profile in other areas. Eventually, the old understanding will fade away—although that can take years. There are still those who believe that I write almost entirely about personal computing, even though less than a third of my writing in the last couple of years has dealt with PC topics.

You may never be able to shake off renown in one area—but you can gain a reputation in other areas. If you're asked to speak about something that no longer interests you, say so and suggest an alternative.

Don't be too quick to dismiss an earlier interest, particularly one where you feel you've said what you have to say. A few years ago, I was asked to write an article on a topic I'd covered in several other articles and a book. I commented that this was sort of old hat, but the editor noted that I hadn't addressed that publication's readers. I put together a new piece covering the key issues in relatively concise form—and the new article, which I almost decided not to write, has been one of my most widely cited articles and won a cash award. You never know.

You can also make light of areas of your persona that you believe to be wrong, and in the process defuse stereotyping and bad feelings. I've found some barbed self-references to be particularly effective, as long as they're followed by clear commentary that leaves little doubt as to my real opinion. Yes, a few people will still get it wrong. That's okay.

All of this has to do with your public persona as a writer and speaker. None of this is who *you* are, of course—unless writing or speaking has moved beyond hobby or avocation to become your passion. If that's the case, I'm not qualified to comment on your situation.

## What's Next?

What comes after success? When you're the best-known writer on one aspect of librarianship, you may wind up teaching on that topic as an adjunct faculty member. Once established, you can almost always revisit the territory in new speeches and reevaluate it for new articles and books. That's worth considering after a few years, particularly if you bring an unusual perspective to the topic. What's changed? What would you have written differently if you were doing it again? Do new audiences need to hear the recent history of the topic—or simply a new focus?

When you work in several areas, have you considered how and whether they fit together? They may not. I still don't see any connection between desktop publishing and the USMARC formats, to name an extreme case. But there might be some—and when you've thought deeply and written extensively about several areas, you're in a great position to spot those connections. You can expand as well as inform the field.

Have your writing skills and observation evolved so much that you should try something entirely different, such as fiction? Were there aspects of topics where you exercised self-censorship for your own good and the good of your employer, but times and your situation have changed?

What did it all mean, particularly your papers and articles that explained the facts and stayed at that level? Why did you persist in areas where nobody else bothered to write, and when you knew you were making more enemies than friends in the process? Did your persistence make sense, or did the world change out from under you?

We probably don't want to hear about the time "this reminds me of," although most of us geezers lapse into reminiscence more often than we should. Sometimes, however, we need to hear lessons from earlier events that we've forgotten in the meantime.

Why should you keep writing and speaking?

Because you still have something to say.

# RESOURCES

This appendix provides information on various resources that library writers may find useful. Electronic resources change rapidly. If the web addresses noted here don't work, use the usual research tools (e.g., Google, AllTheWeb, or AltaVista). The linking proclivity of librarians almost ensures that the desired addresses will appear at or near the top of results in link-rated search engines.

## Web-Based Library Journals, Newsletters, and Zines

Peter Scott's Library Journals, Newsletters, and Zines site (www.libdex. com/journals.html) lists more than 100 library-related publications with some presence on the Internet. It's probably the best place to start looking for author guidelines for magazines and journals, as well as direct links to web-based zines, e-journals, and e-newsletters. Scott includes a number of publications that are dormant or defunct.

Two of the best (and most readily available) examples of contributor guidelines, in addition to the *ITAL* guidelines discussed in chapter 3, are the following:

> *Computers in Libraries* offers explicit guidelines for contributors (www. infotoday.com/cilmag/contrib.htm), along with a detailed FAQ for writers (www.infotoday.com/cilmag/faq.htm). This magazine specifically invites online queries rather than complete articles, includes an editorial calendar with query and article deadlines, specifically says to allow up to a month after the query deadline for response, and notes the payment range for feature articles ($200 to $300). It's one of the clearest and most welcoming sets of contribution guidelines I've seen.

*D-Lib Magazine* also offers clear author guidelines (www.dlib.org/dlib/
author-guidelines.html), including explicit length limitations and
notes on the editorial process. No mention of honoraria appears, and
you should probably not expect payment from this e-magazine.

Four broadly read, currently produced web-based zines and newsletters
that give a sense of the range of such publications are the following:

*Cites & Insights: Crawford at Large* (cites.boisestate.edu or cical.home.
att.net) appears roughly once a month as print-ready PDF issues
announced through a notification mailing list and three library electronic discussion lists (Web4Lib, PACS-L, and PUBLIB). Issues typically range from fourteen to twenty print pages. Each annual volume
ends with an index, but no full-text searching is available. Written by
Walt Crawford, augmented by reader feedback.

*Current Cites* (sunsite.berkeley.edu/CurrentCites/), probably the oldest
continuously published library-related e-newsletter, appears exactly
once a month as e-mailed pure-text issues, each containing ten to fifteen annotated citations of current literature. The website offers
access to the current issue, as well as a link to sign up for the mailing list and searchable access to the citations and those cited articles
that are freely available on the Web. Written by a team of librarians
and library staff.

*Ex Libris* (marylaine.com/exlibris/) appears most Fridays. Each single-
article issue, a straightforward HTML page, is numbered and dated.
The website also offers subject access to past issues, links to Marylaine
Block's other sites, and a set of links to "Guru Interviews" that have
appeared previously in *Ex Libris*. Written by Marylaine Block.

*Library Juice* (libr.org/Juice/) appears "(nearly) every other Wednesday
night." As with *Current Cites,* it appears as pure ASCII text and is
available as an e-mailed subscription or directly on the website.
Edited and published by Rory Litwin, with a mix of his own writing
and contributions from a variety of sources.

## Library Discussion Lists

Library-Oriented Lists & Electronic Serials (liblists.wrlc.org) has been built
and maintained since 1990 and continues to be the best place to begin

exploring electronic discussion lists in the library field. It's also another good resource for zines and e-journals.

## Library Weblogs

The indefatigable Peter Scott also maintains Library Weblogs (www.libdex. com/weblogs.html), a list that includes more than eighty weblogs (as of December 2002) from nine countries. As usual with Scott's work, it's probably the best single place to begin exploring library weblogs—which are a tiny and (generally) relatively formal subset of the weblog universe.

The following weblogs, listed alphabetically because my priorities may not be yours, may or may not be representative of the field but do show some of the range. These are all weblogs that I check periodically. You should read some of these and some other weblogs before you start your own; you may decide to participate in one of the group efforts such as LISNews. You'll find sidebar links to other weblogs at many of these sites, providing an even wider range of examples. Note that I do not use the word "opinionated" in any negative sense; it's an attempt to describe, not judge.

> Bibliolatry (www.etches-johnson.com/bibliolatry/), a Canadian weblog, typically includes four to six briefly annotated links in each post, with posts every few days. Amanda Etches-Johnson's annotations are sometimes cryptic (and frequently opinionated), but the selections are intriguing.

> BookNews (futureofthebook.com) is Gary Frost's log on the "preservation and persistence of the changing book." Don't expect daily postings; do expect lengthy, idiosyncratic discussions of items posted, with illustrations and links to commentary and reports.

> FOS News (www.earlham.edu/~peters/fos/fosblog.html) is edited and mostly written by Peter Suber, a key figure in the free online scholarship (FOS) movement, although there are other contributors. New postings appear almost every day, typically two to six extensively annotated links with more argumentation than straight opinion. The site also links to other FOS-related sites.

> L.A.C.K. (www.conk.com/zed/lack/) is short for "Librarians Are Corrupting Kids," a charming name for Chris Zammarelli's links on censorship, filtering, and related topics. The number and frequency of postings vary widely; annotations can be cryptic but are generally clear and charmingly frank.

librarian.net (www.librarian.net) comes from Jessamyn West, "rarin' librarian," who has variously described herself as an anarchist librarian and radical librarian. She selects two to six items two or three times a week, providing short but clear annotations for linked items.

LibraryNotes (www.librarynotes.net) generally includes relatively few items with fairly long annotations from Sandra Clockedile.

LibraryPlanet (www.libraryplanet.com) also offers relatively few items and provides long, frequently opinionated annotations. The complex site appears to be a group effort, headed by Michael Pate, and includes links to other sites in a number of areas, not just librarianship.

Library Stuff (www.librarystuff.net) is a classic weblog from Steven M. Cohen that includes the online library cartoon "Overdue" at the top of the page. Cohen covers a wide range, generally adding several items each day. He tends to separate description from opinion, an unusual methodology, and (as with a number of other weblogs) explicitly invites and automatically posts comments from readers.

LISNews (lisnews.com) is a group effort headed by Blake Carver. Each item usually comes with a full paragraph description, sometimes but not always idiosyncratic, and frequently with even more commentary behind a local link. Several items usually appear each day—so many that entries are archived weekly or more often. The site supports comments (and gets quite a few of them) and includes occasional polls; the archive (more than 5,600 stories as of December 2002) can be searched or browsed by topic. (Many other weblogs also have searchable archives.)

New Pages (www.newpages.com/weblog/) points to "alternatives in print and media," with substantial sets of posts added each Monday, Wednesday, and Friday. Casey Hill runs this impressive weblog. Annotations tend to quote portions of the linked story.

Peter Scott's Library Blog (www.lights.com/scott/) is Peter Scott's own weblog (and another Canadian weblog). He cites newsletters, databases, upcoming conferences, and other items available on the Web; the brief annotations are typically neutral in tone.

The ResourceShelf (www.resourceshelf.com) is sometimes also known as "VAS&ND." Gary Price posts detailed descriptions for these links, which primarily deal with new electronic resources and related issues.

Scholarly Electronic Publishing Weblog (info.lib.uh.edu/sepb/sepw.htm) comes from Charles W. Bailey Jr. and offers clearly described links to a wide range of articles and e-publications in the broad area described by the title. Bailey typically provides two to six (or more) items each day, occasionally with an explicit recommendation but generally with a neutral description. Omit the last segment of the URL and you'll get to Bailey's *Scholarly Electronic Publishing Bibliography,* a first-rate ongoing e-publication.

The Shifted Librarian (www.theshiftedlibrarian.com) sometimes seems overwhelming in its activity and the length of Jenny Levine's annotations, which typically combine selective quotation with her clear commentary.

## Library Book Publishers

All publishers noted here provide e-mail and postal addresses for appropriate contacts at their websites. You'll find that their author guidelines are generally similar, but each publisher has distinctive preferences in regard to the form of proposals and whether proposals should be preceded by query letters or e-mail.

ALA Editions offers author proposal guidelines and an extensive FAQ section at www.ala.org/editions/forauthors/. The publisher does thirty-five to forty projects each year (primarily books) and prefers two- to three-page proposals, but will consider completed manuscripts (query first). The FAQ is fascinating. Allow six to eight weeks for evaluation.

Greenwood Press has a page for prospective authors at www.greenwood. com/author/, including details on preparing a proposal. The site does not indicate a review period.

Information Today has book proposal guidelines at www.infotoday. com/books/proposal.shtml. This publisher prefers printed proposals and attempts to respond within four weeks of receipt.

Libraries Unlimited offers manuscript proposal guidelines at www.lu.com; click on the "Manuscript Submissions" link. This publisher requests an e-mail review prior to proposal submission.

McFarland & Company's guidelines are at www.mcfarlandpub. com/book_proposals.html. These guidelines cover all of McFarland, which publishes nonfiction in a wide range of areas. McFarland welcomes query letters, full proposals, or even complete manuscripts; attempts to answer queries "within a few days"; and prefers to operate via print mail—"a paper copy makes a better impression." It usually responds to full proposals within a month.

Neal-Schuman Publishers provides brief guidelines at www.neal-schuman.com/submission.html. The page does not indicate a review period.

Scarecrow Press has guidelines at www.scarecrowpress.com/SCP/ Submission/. Scarecrow prefers a proposal to a completed manuscript, and takes two to four months to review proposals.

# BIBLIOGRAPHY

*The Chicago Manual of Style.* 14th ed. Chicago: University of Chicago Press, 1993.

Crawford, Walt. "Building a Serials Key Word Index." *Journal of Library Automation* 9 (March 1976): 34–47.

———. "The E-Files: E-Newsletters and E-Zines: From Current Cites to NewBreed Librarian." *American Libraries* 32 (December 2001): 51–53.

———. "The E-Files: Library Lists: Building on E-Mail." *American Libraries* 32 (November 2001): 56–58.

———. "The E-Files: 'You *Must* Read This': Library Weblogs." *American Libraries* 32 (October 2001): 74–76.

———. "Give Me a Break!" *EContent* 25 (April 2002): 42–43.

———. "Long Searches, Slow Response: Recent Experience on RLIN." *Information Technology and Libraries* 2 (June 1983): 176–82.

———. *MARC for Library Use: Understanding the USMARC Formats.* White Plains, N.Y.: Knowledge Industry Publications, 1984.

Crawford, Walt, and Michael Gorman. *Future Libraries: Dreams, Madness, and Reality.* Chicago: American Library Association, 1995.

Hall, Danelle. "A View from the Back Wall." *American Libraries* 33 (May 2002): 64–65.

*ITAL* Instructions to Authors. Available at http://www.lita.org/ital/infoauth. htm (accessed 6 June 2002).

Plotnik, Arthur. *The Elements of Expression.* New York: Holt, 1996.

Strunk, William, Jr., and E. B. White. *The Elements of Style.* 3rd ed. New York: Macmillan, 1979.

# INDEX

**WALT CRAWFORD** is a senior analyst at RLG in Mountain View, California. He has published fourteen books (including this one) and more than 300 articles and columns on libraries, technology, media, publishing, and personal computing. He also speaks to library groups a few times a year. Crawford currently writes "The Crawford Files" in *American Libraries,* the "disContent" column in *EContent,* and the "PC Monitor" column in *Online.* He also writes and publishes *Cites & Insights: Crawford at Large,* a web-distributed zine.